A PASSION FOR HORSES

True Stories of Lives Lived Loving Horses

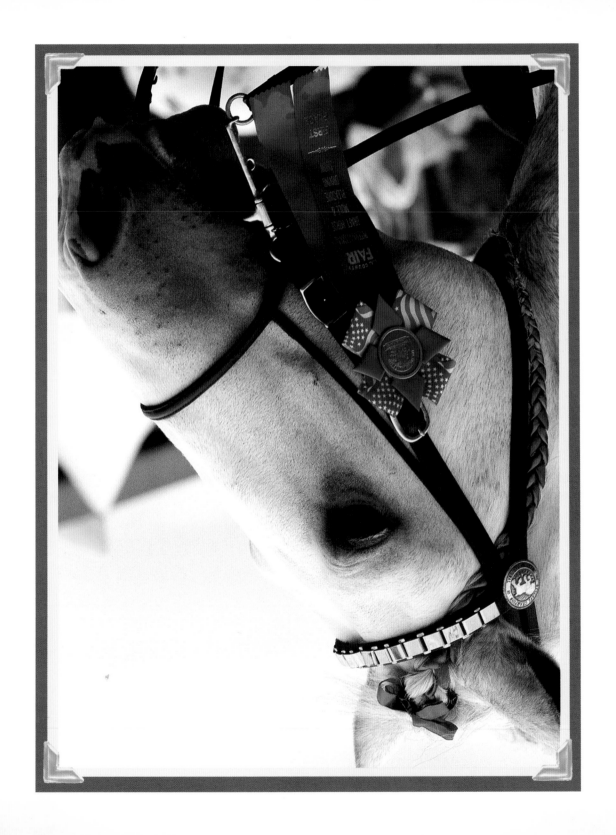

A PASSION FOR HORSES

True Stories of Lives Lived Loving Horses

BY CINDY HALE

PHOTOGRAPHS BY SHARON P. FIBELKORN

BOWTIE
PRESS®

A DIVISION OF BOWTIE, INC.
IRVINE, CALIFORNIA

Karla Austin, Business Operations Manager
Ruth Strother, Editor-At-Large
Erin Kuechenmeister, Production Editor
Rebekah Bryant, Editorial Assistant

Nick Clemente, Special Consultant
Jen Dorsey, Associate Editor
Michelle Martinez, Assistant Editor
Bocu & Bocu, Book Design

The photograph on page 103 is provided by Cheryl Walker © 2002

Library of Congress Cataloging-in-Publication Data

Hale, Cindy.
  A passion for horses : true stories of lives lived loving horses / by Cindy Hale ;
photographs by Sharon P. Fibelkorn.
    p. cm.
  ISBN 1-931993-33-5 (soft cover : alk. paper)
  1. Horses—United States—Anecdotes. 2. Horsemen and
horsewomen—United States—Anecdotes. 3. Human–animal
communication—United States—Anecdotes. I. Title.
SF301.H35 2003
636.1'3'0973--dc21

2003012795

BowTie Press®
A Division of BowTie, Inc.
3 Burroughs
Irvine, California 92618

Printed and Bound in Singapore
10 9 8 7 6 5 4 3 2 1

For my sister Jill:
Through the many years of sharing ponies
Competing for blue ribbons
And nurturing foals
Your wit and insight
Have helped keep alive my passion for horses

Contents

Preface 9

Acknowledgments 11

CHAPTER 1   A Home for Unwanted Racehorses   13

CHAPTER 2   A Kingdom of Carousel Horses   23

CHAPTER 3   Cut from the Heart of Texas   31

CHAPTER 4   In the Land of Giants   39

CHAPTER 5   My Afternoon with Wilma   47

CHAPTER 6   Joy   55

CHAPTER 7   The View from the Back of a Horse   61

CHAPTER 8   Bronzed Beauties   65

CHAPTER 9   In All Fairness   71

CHAPTER 10   The Horse of a Lifetime   77

CHAPTER 11   Rides Well with Others   83

CHAPTER 12   On Parade   91

CHAPTER 13   Ponies of Our Past   99

CHAPTER 14   Click!   103

CHAPTER 15   Up in the Air   109

CHAPTER 16   The Wonder Horse   115

CHAPTER 17   A Member of the Family   123

CHAPTER 18   All the Pretty (Model) Horses   131

CHAPTER 19   A Winning Combination   139

CHAPTER 20   Girls and Their Horses   145

CHAPTER 21   Lassoing Life's Lessons   149

CHAPTER 22   A Life Spent with Horses   157

Preface

While I was reorganizing a photo album, I realized I was not getting any younger. As I flipped from page to page, there was no ignoring that I had become taller, leaner, and more wrinkled. But what impressed me even more was that every page of the album featured at least one photo of me with a horse. Better yet, I could still recall each animal's name, his quirks, and what it felt like to sit his trot or caress his neck. I think that photo album best defines my life. Even the earliest pictures, just grainy black-and-white snapshots, show that I was a girl in love with anything connected to horses. You can tell by how proudly I modeled my cowgirl outfit at age four.

Over the years, I've learned that horse lovers share three things. First, we need little prodding to converse about how horses have impacted our lives, regardless of the differences in our ages, geographical locales, or financial underpinnings. Second, horse lovers have a habit of collecting photographs. Thank goodness for snapshots that help us recall a treasured pony, a faithful show horse, or a long lost riding companion. Finally, horse people are an expressive bunch. Our love of horses is so strong, so ingrained in the very essence of our soul, that we seek out ways to express that love.

A Passion for Horses profiles people who have unique ways of telling the rest of the world about their love affair with horses. It also is a collection of my personal reflections after spending years in the saddle. But most of all, *A Passion for Horses* is a book for kindred spirits who feel a special stirring in their hearts whenever they look into the deep, liquid eyes of that magnificent creature, the horse.

Acknowledgments

I'm still impressed by how much is involved with actually getting a book to market. My friends and acquaintances in the worlds of writing and publishing helped guide me as I wrote *A Passion for Horses*. I thank them for their honesty and support.

There are two very special people I want to acknowledge. One of those people is my husband, Ron. I'm still not convinced he understands my own passion for horses. However, throughout more than 20 years of marriage, he has graciously made room in our relationship for a small herd of well-indulged equines.

The other person is Sharon Fibelkorn, my photographer. Not only is she a gifted artist, she's also a good sport. I'm sure I've ruined countless weekends for her by scheduling photo shoots at parades, racetracks, horse shows, and stables. Fortunately, she has always had more enthusiasm for my writing projects than she expressed toward riding the pony her father bestowed upon her at age six, as demonstrated in this snapshot.

A Home for Unwanted Racehorses

In another lifetime, Helen Meredith's jade green eyes and prominent cheekbones would've earned her a role as a cover girl. But instead of modeling, she chose to spend her life in the world of racehorses first as an exercise rider, then as an assistant trainer, and eventually as a winning jockey. Now those patrician facial features are bronzed and etched by years spent outdoors, staring down the backstretch from atop the back of a galloping Thoroughbred. And those deep green eyes can seem as tempestuous as the chilly waters that surround her Scottish homeland.

Helen, it seems, is much like one of the headstrong Thoroughbreds she's worked with for over three decades. She is, aptly speaking, currently bucking the system. In 1992 she founded the United Pegasus Foundation, whose laudable yet lofty belief is that "no Thoroughbred should be denied a second career or a dignified retirement." This philosophy puts her at odds with some of her peers in the racing industry where horses are often seen as commodities. She believes that many sore and injured horses are kept running, even if that means dropping them down a peg in class or shipping them to a cheaper circuit of tracks. The geldings—castrated male horses—are the most victimized in this scenario because they have no future in the breeding shed. When they are too crippled to race or be retrained as saddle horses, they often end up at the slaughterhouse.

Helen's goal with the United Pegasus Foundation is to change the mind-set of owners and trainers so they stop running a horse before he becomes hopelessly unsound. The foundation serves as a foster home for those Thoroughbreds who still have a chance at another life. This unsettles those in the business who accuse her of putting a tawdry spin on horse racing. After all, it's likely better public relations to

focus on the latest Kentucky Derby winner than to force racing fans to contemplate just what happens to the thousands of Thoroughbreds who rarely find their way to the winner's circle. Some have even chided her for wanting to warehouse lame, useless geldings, questioning why she seeks funds for a pension plan so equine lawn ornaments can lounge in a pasture. "Nobody wants to warehouse them," Helen says incredulously, shaking her head at that remark. "I certainly don't want to. I wish I could find them all homes. If the owners and trainers would just take responsibility for

Opposite: Helen Meredith, founder of United Pegasus Foundation, started working with horses when she was 15. Above: A Pegasus dog guards the hay.

these horses, if they wouldn't race them until they're unusable for any sort of riding, there wouldn't be this problem."

Helen's passion for the plight of racehorses stems from her personal history. The story of how she turned her devotion to animals into a full-time job begins with a tale that's not so uncommon—a young girl in love with horses.

Helen was born in Scotland to a working-class family. Her first recollection of riding was when she was just four or five years old. Gypsy caravans would wind their way through her village at regular intervals. In those days, the nomadic clans were known for their fine horses and handcrafted wares. While camped in the nearby meadows and forests, the gypsies would tether their horses to low posts so they could graze. Helen recalls making regular detours with her brothers on their way home from school and "borrowing" the gypsies' horses for bareback rides.

When her family moved to the steel-working town of Corby, England, Helen made a habit of seeking out anyone who owned a horse or pony so she could get more riding experience. "If anybody had a horse, I'd try to figure out a way to get to ride it." England has long been a culture imbued with horses, so it wasn't unusual that Helen's extended family included a smattering of jockeys and racehorse trainers. These long-distance connections seemed ripe for the horse-crazy Helen to manipulate, but even her grandfather who was a trainer advised anyone in the family against such a career. "He always said it was seven days a week, a lot of work, no thanks, and very little money."

That didn't deter Helen's aspirations, however. "I was always bugging my parents to let me go work with horses," she says, recalling that she was 15 when they relented. "During the Easter vacation break from school, they arranged with some old family friends for me to live with them while I'd go work with racehorses. I know my parents thought, 'Well, this'll

be it. She'll have to get up early in the morning, and that's going to sicken her, and that'll be the end of the whole horse story.'" Of course nothing could be further from the truth, even though Helen's horse career didn't begin glamorously. "I went to the stable and had a quick lesson before the boss got there. It was mostly about how to get on, because they [the racehorses] have these little saddles, so you can't get on yourself, because the saddle will slip, so you have to get a leg up."

The rest of the impromptu lesson consisted of learning how to hold the reins, Helen tells me, nearly laughing at the futility of the hasty session. There were no lofty insights into how to steer a rambunctious racehorse, no tips on finessing her precarious position atop the high-strung horse. She says she was quickly shown how a jockey folds the reins across a horse's neck to brace against the surge of a 1,000-pound beast. The lesson concluded with, "and away you go!"

Away she went indeed, and not always gracefully. Helen puts her hands momentarily over her eyes. "Yeah, the first day I fell off. The stirrups were so short, and I wasn't used to it, so I lost my balance. I didn't feel anything when I came off, but that night my ankle swelled up so badly I couldn't get my boots on the next morning."

Despite the initial calamity, Helen was hooked. When her mother called at the end of her two-week trial, she

Opposite: Many retired racehorses end up at Pegasus.
Left: Helen spent years in Europe honing her riding skills.

realized the plan for her daughter had backfired. "I asked if I could stay another week," Helen says.

Helen not only stayed another week, she never left the world of Thoroughbred racing. She spent years as a "lad," the European term for the exercise riders who groom horses and muck stalls when they aren't working horses. As she traveled the major racetracks of England, Ireland, and France, she became a dependable and savvy assistant trainer. Eventually she ended up in America, having made her first trips accompanying European-trained horses owned by Texas oil billionaire and silver tycoon Nelson Bunker Hunt.

In the late 1980s, Helen settled in the United States and became increasingly aware of how often a racehorse, particularly a gelding, was run past his prime until the owner decided to "get rid of him," a phrase Helen says now with a bitter tone to her heavily accented voice.

In 1989 Helen met and married California racehorse trainer Derek Meredith, and she helped him train the 1993 Breeders' Cup Sprint champion, Cardmania. But it was in 1991, while watching a newscast out of Los Angeles that featured a weeklong series on the slaughtering of horses for human consumption, that Helen found her calling. She was horrified to realize that many of the horses being shoved into cramped cattle trucks and shipped across state lines to be slaughtered were Thoroughbred geldings culled from the racetrack. "I couldn't imagine that some of the very horses I might've worked with were sent to slaughter." That was the genesis of the United Pegasus Foundation, also known as simply Pegasus.

Helen aligned herself with a group of kindhearted, generous Thoroughbred racehorse owners, a smattering of Hollywood celebrities, and a collection of dedicated horse lovers who helped her organize and realize her dream. Through fundraisers and public donations, Pegasus has

become the premier nonprofit charitable home for unwanted racehorses, and Helen is the chief spokesperson, ranch manager, and occasional stall mucker. Thanks to its benefactors, Pegasus now operates two sites. One is a ranch in Northern California for equine pensioners. This is a retirement haven for horses deemed unfit for future use generally due to some sort of devastating injury. The second site is a rehabilitation and adoption center, a foster home for horses, in the southern region. There the new arrivals rest and are brought back to riding condition, and then restarted under saddle for prospective buyers. The horses are priced modestly. Income is used to pay operating costs and maintain the care of the other equine residents.

Currently both ranches are full, housing a total of about one hundred horses. A visit to Pegasus's home in Southern California is like a venture to any well-run horse farm. Here the horses seem unusually tranquil and at ease.

Opposite: The horses at Pegasus nuzzle and get along well with one another.
Above: Pathways at Pegasus are named after inhabitants.

"I tell people,
never get
involved with
a nonprofit
if you've got
an ego."

– HELEN MEREDITH

The back paddock of the adoption facility serves as the community center for a group of geldings. At first glance, the big-bodied horses are fat and sleek. Docile to a fault, they nuzzle visitors and commingle in relative harmony. A horseman would be able to tell that they are a well-bred lot: as a group they are 16-hands tall or more, with necks and shoulders that slope like those of a greyhound. But a quick study of their legs reveals a variety of disabilities. There have bowed tendons, mangled suspensories, and swollen joints.

Helen introduces me to the two elder statesmen of the geldings. One is Music Merci, a silvery gray gelding with a grossly misshapen front leg—the result of too many races on weakened ligaments and a lack of diligent aftercare. Fortunately he was rescued from a dubious end and brought to Pegasus. Not a glorious way for a horse who won over $1.5 million to spend his golden years, but it is better than being on someone's dinner table. The other head honcho is Forty Niner Days. He earned just over $1 million for his owners but is now unusable for anything other than service as a four-legged pasture pet, dozing in the sun.

Helen walks among the band of retirees, laying a hand on each warm, dusty neck. She gives each one a pat, and calls him by name. She can recite the peculiarities of each personality, the nature of his physical disability, and the often-incredible story of his journey from the winner's circle to obscurity. Some of these horses, perhaps due to their fame, will luck into a patron who will sponsor their care with a tax-deductible monthly stipend. Others draw their pension from a general fund made up of contributions. Younger, less seriously injured geldings are rested, doctored, and schooled under saddle for new jobs, many as English show horses.

But regardless of the efforts of Pegasus, Helen says there are always more horses to be rescued. When asked if the task sometimes seems insurmountable, her Scottish brogue returns in full force and those green eyes narrow. "For sure, I forever worry where the next dime is coming from," she admits. She scoffs at the notion that not having the full support of the racing industry is stressful. "I tell people, never get involved with a nonprofit if you've got an ego."

Ego is not required. But a heart certainly is.

Opposite: Helen knows each horse's story. Above: A beautiful day at Pegasus.

2

A KINGDOM OF CAROUSEL HORSES

There is something about Lourinda Bray's facial expressions and joyful demeanor that elicit thoughts of pixies and elves and a mythical other world. It seems appropriate that each day she spends most of her waking hours inside a warehouse near Pasadena, California, that is stocked with 285 vintage carousel horses in various stages of restoration. Her magical task is to return these grand old steeds to their former glory.

It is a wondrous world, this cavelike setting where a kingdom of ornately carved horses are paused in mid-gallop, their nostrils flared, their forelocks flipped back against the wind. Lourinda's herd of horses stretches from one end of the concrete-and-metal building to the other. The first horses to catch a visitor's eye are those whose layers of old enamel have been stripped away and now look naked in their natural brown wood. But then the lure of the restored horses becomes captivating, with their gilt-edged saddles, jeweled breast collars, and ornate floral embellishments. Who can ignore horses that are lavishly decorated with hand-carved monkeys clinging to their withers or metallic green serpents coiled around the cantle of their

Opposite: Lourinda Bray spends hundreds of hours painstakingly refurbishing each horse. Left: Carousel horses after paint removal.

handsome black horse sporting medieval battle armor has been christened Zeus. The horses from England often come supplied with their own names. The English had a habit of naming their carousel mounts, often painting the monikers on a banner just beneath the mane. It was easy to spy Trevor and Quirk, who were at the midpoint of their rebirth. Lourinda gestures toward another British import that has yet to be restored. "See that banner on his neck?" Currently only a mishmash of scrollwork decorates the ribbon. "Once I get down to the original paint, I'll discover his name. It'll still be there."

If you imagine Lourinda to be someone who just took a fancy to merry-go-round horses and began a hobby painting pretty colors on them, you're mistaken. She holds a B.A. in painting and an M.A. in theater with an emphasis on set design. Plus she is a veritable walking, talking encyclopedia on the history of carousels. With little prodding, she can recite the names of the handful of craftsmen who came to America at the start of the twentieth century, bringing with them the artistry of hand-carved wooden carousel horses. M.C. Illions, for example, was of Russian descent. His horses are distinguished in part by their ornate gilt manes and each animal's unique-ness. An American-born carver, Allan Herschell, is known for the similarities of his horses as well as the wide variety of his horses' trappings. Lourinda currently has 74 Allan Herschell steeds in her stable.

Of course, Lourinda is also an expert in the construction—and the near destruction—of carousel horses. "The body of the wooden carousel horse is basically just a hollow box, a rectangle like a shoebox," she explains. "The rest of it is solid wood." Since many of the horses date from around 1920, the restoration process includes extensive surgery. Besides a skilled carver who tediously

saddles?'" "It never gets old to me," Lourinda says, her eyes dancing with delight beneath bangs of curly brown hair. "Each day before I start working, the first thing I do is walk around and see everybody," she says, referring to her attentive horses who, indeed, seem poised to whinny.

That she eventually names every new arrival is evidence of her attachment to each horse. A few will soon be christened with surnames reflecting the amusement park from which they originated, such as Paradise Park or Playland. Others are bequeathed mythical names. One

Above: Lourinda either discovers a horse's name in the many layers of paint or christens him with a new name.

Opposite: One of Lourinda's horses in transition.

removes any dry rot, she has just one other employee at her Running Horse Studio outside Pasadena, California. The restoration process is a time-consuming labor of true love. "First we have to take apart the horse and remove all the old glue from the joints. Then any missing parts—on a really prime piece there won't be any—must be recarved and replaced. Nails rust, so they're removed and replaced with small wooden dowels. Finally," she says with a sigh and an elfin smile, "we strip off the old paint. And there is always a lot of old paint."

There is so much old paint because once the horse becomes part of a machine (the term for the actual merry-go-round) the workers at the park or carnival have little time for recrafting any damage. Instead they just apply another coat of paint. "Some horses have as much as 20 layers of paint," she says, then pats the neck of one creamy white prancing stallion. "On this one, when I reached, oh, about layer 14, I suddenly found this area that was still sticky and sweet-smelling. Being the curious person that I am, I dabbed my finger in it and took a taste. Sure enough, it tasted like some kind of syrup, maybe even cherry-flavored. I'm thinking what happened was about 50 years ago a child riding this horse spilled her drink on its neck and some more paint was slapped on to cover up the stain." The layers of paint reveal the secrets of the horses' pasts, making Lourinda a detective of sorts.

Another such mystery led to a change in restoration tactics. Arguably the most exquisite horse, which was black with ornate saddlery, was painstakingly restored. "Restoration means you go back to the beginning, to the original look," Lourinda explains. "So here we spend all this time and work getting this beautiful creature back to how it originally was. Then one day three years later, I'm admiring it and I notice this telltale little pile

"Once I get down to the original paint, I'll discover his name. If it still be there."

– LOURINDA BRAY

of wood dust underneath it on the floor." She rolls her eyes and says the dreaded word: "Termites." So the poor horse had to undergo an entire makeover. And what did she learn? "Well, we had to fumigate the entire warehouse. That was a nightmare! Now we have a separate trailer outside and every new horse gets fumigated before it comes in here."

Lourinda's ultimate goal is to open a carousel museum that is both educational and entertaining. She certainly has the stable of horses to equip a large machine. While the horses are scarce vestiges from nearly a century ago, they are not an endangered species. Yet. "There were 4,000 active carousels in America in the 1930s. Each machine had approximately 36 horses on it, some had as many as 54," explains Lourinda. That means at one time, there were at least 150,000 hand-carved wooden carousel horses galloping away on merry-go-rounds. Those hardy ones that have survived merely need someone like Lourinda to give them new life.

Lourinda doesn't give new life just to wooden horses— she has a penchant for doing the same to the living, breathing variety. Perhaps it's maternal instinct that drives her, a need to nurture something. Or maybe it's simply that force within every artist that compels her to coax beauty out of the rough elements of her chosen media. But the same passion Lourinda brings to her profession led her to buy a live horse named Bare Facts over 20 years ago.

The gelding had suffered horrible injuries from wrestling with a barbed wire fence, and his owner sold him to Lourinda for the grand sum of one dollar with the disclaimer that he might not fully recover. Ever faithful, Lourinda nursed Bare Facts through an entire year of recuperation. The two of them bonded, and they enjoyed years of trail riding.

Each year, when the bay grew a thick winter coat, Lourinda would shave his wooly body and keep him cozy with a plush blanket. True to her artistic nature, she'd embellish the haircut by leaving some ornate pattern in his original hair coat. One year he sported a dragon on his haunch. Another year he bore the trappings of a carousel horse. With such loving care, the one-dollar horse lived to be 31 years old. It's obvious Lourinda still misses him. "I painted my very first carousel horse to look like him, a bright red bay," she says fondly. That first horse was purchased in 1980, when Bare Facts was still a youngster. "When I was a child, I loved to ride the carousel," she says. "I always thought that the greatest job in the world would be to paint the horses."

Now that Lourinda's youthful dream has been realized in glorious fashion, perhaps she'll find another real-life horse to capture her heart. Until then, she'll reside among her kingdom of carousel horses.

Opposite: Lourinda's goal is to open a carousel museum. Above: Bare Facts, Lourinda's first horse, has been the inspiration for her work with carousel mounts.

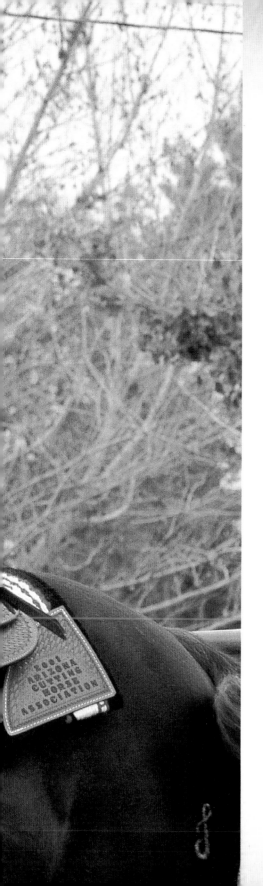

CUT FROM
THE HEART OF TEXAS

aving dinner with Colleen Voight is like sitting across the table from a Texas twister. She is so full of energy that the overhead lights threaten to dim in honor of her vibrancy. About 5 feet 10 inches in her boots, she has a mane of sorrel-colored hair, which she tosses back over her shoulders as she leans forward and squints her blue eyes with an intensity much like the cutting horses she rides. Colleen is ready to get down to business and talk about horses. Her voice is sweetened by her native Texan accent and frequently punctuated with a laugh unbridled by concerns for the tame aloofness of the other diners.

Colleen is no demure equestrienne. She's not content to be propped upon a sedate western pleasure horse. Instead, she cuts cattle aboard her small, wiry gelding named Rum 'n' Tari. Cutting is an exercise born of Texas ranchland, where a chosen steer (perhaps one requiring doctoring or branding) is separated, or cut, from the herd. The bovine's natural impulse is to return to his clan. The quarter horse, with training that nurtures an innate drive to work a steer, is determined to prevent that from happening. What ensues is a fast, rollicking battle of wits and brawn as horse and steer go head-to-head until the steer surrenders. Cutting is in Colleen's life's blood. In 2001, she won both a world championship and a reserve championship from the National Cutting Horse Association, and is continuing her quest for another title.

We stop chatting just long enough to order dinner. I notice the young server can't transcribe our requests as fast as we make them, pausing to rescribble his notes. He must think he is being cut and cornered himself. When he steps away from the vortex of energy that seems to hover over our table, Colleen begins her tale of life on horseback.

She spent her childhood in Star, Texas, where her father managed a cattle ranch in the tiny community, which she describes with a wink as "very country." The one-room school she attended was set in the middle of a cattle pasture. When I raise my eyebrows at that, she says with mock indignity, "Well, there was a road. And there was a fence around the schoolhouse." She reveals that there were a grand total of 68 students from kindergarten through high school. And yes, cattle ran around outside. With a note of fondness she says, "If my dad was out working cows at lunchtime, he'd tie his horse up to the fence and eat with us."

Because horses were part of daily life on a ranch, Colleen can't remember a time when she didn't ride. Mostly it was her grandfather who taught her the basics of how to hold the reins and how to sit in the saddle. "Maybe that's why I ride the way he did, why I have his presence on the back of a horse," she remarks. Though she'd ridden

Opposite: Cutting champion Colleen Voight can't remember a time when she didn't ride. Above: Colleen in action.

some of the quarter horses on the ranch, as a little girl she struggled with their size. So one day her father brought home a small Shetland pony he'd rescued because he wasn't being treated well. "He thought he was doing both me and the pony a favor," Colleen recalls. "He said, 'Shorty needs a good home.' But the little thing bucked me off every chance it got!" Colleen laughs at the irony. Why is it that ponies often conspire to create chaos?

At that moment the server, with obvious trepidation, presents us with our dinner. Between stabbing bites of pasta, Colleen relates the story of her very first horse, Dudley. "He was a very fancy bay colt, a grandson of Doc

Bar [a famous sire of cutting horses]. My sister and I could ride Dudley all over the ranch, bareback, double, whatever. He was the sweetest horse." But one summer day, the two girls conjured up a plan to have some cowgirl fun. "My dad had ridden bucking horses when we were very little, so it was only natural that my sister and I wanted to try it. We dragged out some corral panels and built a bucking chute. Then we figured we'd have some fun with Dudley by tightening up the back cinch, the flank strap, on the western stock saddle. Even though Dudley was very gentle, as soon as we buckled the flank strap, he'd start bucking. We'd take turns trying to buck him out, trying to ride him. He'd buck us off, we'd fall off in the dirt, and then we'd do it again."

I ask her if her parents knew their Doc Bar grandson was being bucked out by their aspiring rodeo queens. "Well, not until my mother looked out into the back pasture and saw us." Colleen becomes animated with the recollection. "She came just running out," she says, waving her hands expressively. "My sister and I were so proud that we could make Dudley buck, like we had discovered his hidden talent. We thought he was really good at it. Our mother," she says, lowering her head and her voice, "wasn't real happy with us."

Colleen's first real introduction to the world of competitive cutting came when she was in first grade. "My mother took me out of school to go to Fort Worth for the national cutting horse futurity. I helped my relatives decorate their horses' stalls. I remember I went over to the arena and sat on the fence and watched the cutters loping their horses down at one end and working cattle at the other end." She pauses and seems almost wistful. I suddenly became aware of the restaurant's din around us. Thoughtfully she says, "If you've never been to the Will Rogers Coliseum, it's just this incredible place. It's an indoor arena, so it's an intimate setting, but the atmosphere, even the smell, is unlike any other arena. There's this whole mystique associated with it, because they've been doing cutting there since the early 40s. There's just such a heritage, so much history. To me it felt like I was inside a castle. I remember thinking, 'I am going to do this one day.'"

It wasn't until she was 18, however, that she rode her first real cutting horse. The occasion played out like a Texan rite of passage. "My grandfather put me on his great little mare named Holly. She was only about 14.1 hands, but she was just this wonderful cutting mare. I remember riding out to the herd and I pushed a cow out. You have to understand,"

"And just
today I was
wondering
how I could
bedazzle my
name down
the pant leg
of my jeans."

– COLLEEN VOIGHT

Colleen emphasizes, her blue eyes narrowing in earnest, "I had wanted to ride a real cutting horse since I was 6 years old. I had been imagining this moment for 12 years. Well," she says, shaking her head and laughing quietly, "Holly made about four moves and my granddad said, 'Okay! That's enough.' Now that I know more about cutting that was probably all his heart could handle, seeing me on his prized mare, no doubt out of control. Of course, I remember it being fun. And beautiful."

Colleen has much more expertise in cutting these days. Her granddad would be proud. Last year she was on the road two hundred days with her horse, a necessity to earn enough points in competition to win a title. Most of the time, she travels with Rum 'n' Tari and her Jack Russell terrier, Milo. Her longest one-way haul to date was to Fort Klamath, Oregon. "It was 15 hours of straight driving," she sighs.

One of her two biggest supporters is her husband, who doesn't ride but who encourages Colleen every step of the way. And then there's her trainer and coach Bill Martin, whom Colleen describes as "a legend in the world of cutting. We're both overachievers. Even if I win a class, Bill can tell me a way to do it better next time."

Yet it's Colleen's spirit, that undeniable cowgirl spunk that compels her to keep cutting. "I feel as if I've found my people!" she declares, then offers that even as a schoolgirl in Texas she often felt out of place. "I never really fit in, except that I had a few girlfriends who really loved horses, too. You know," she says, "I am a girly girl, and I love being a girly girl." As evidence she displays her beautifully manicured nails. I can't help but notice that one hand sports a large ring of a horse head encircled by a diamond-encrusted horseshoe. "But I don't mind getting dirty and doing ranch work with cattle and horses."

When I joke that it seems that horses and cows and the whole rip-snortin' world of cutting seems to pervade

her entire persona, Colleen shakes off any offense with a toss of that auburn hair. "My nonhorsey friends will joke, if I go to loan them anything to wear, 'Now, does this have any marabou plumes on it, or rhinestones, or is it leopard print?' Because even the stuff I wear when I'm cutting is, well, different. I'll cut with a couple of feathers in my hair and something sparkly on." She catches me laughing. "I know. I probably look like I came from a square dance."

"But do you own a Be-Dazzler?" I ask in my best investigative reporter voice, referring to the little gun used by crafters to rivet rhinestones onto garments. Colleen smacks her palms down on the tablecloth in amazement, thrilled to have discovered someone who was familiar with the oft-maligned device. "Why yes, I do own a Be-Dazzler," she says proudly. In a full-hearted Texan twang she laughs, "And just today I was wondering how I could bedazzle my name down the pant leg of my jeans."

Opposite and above: Colleen competes with her gelding, Rum 'n' Tari.

IN THE LAND OF GIANTS

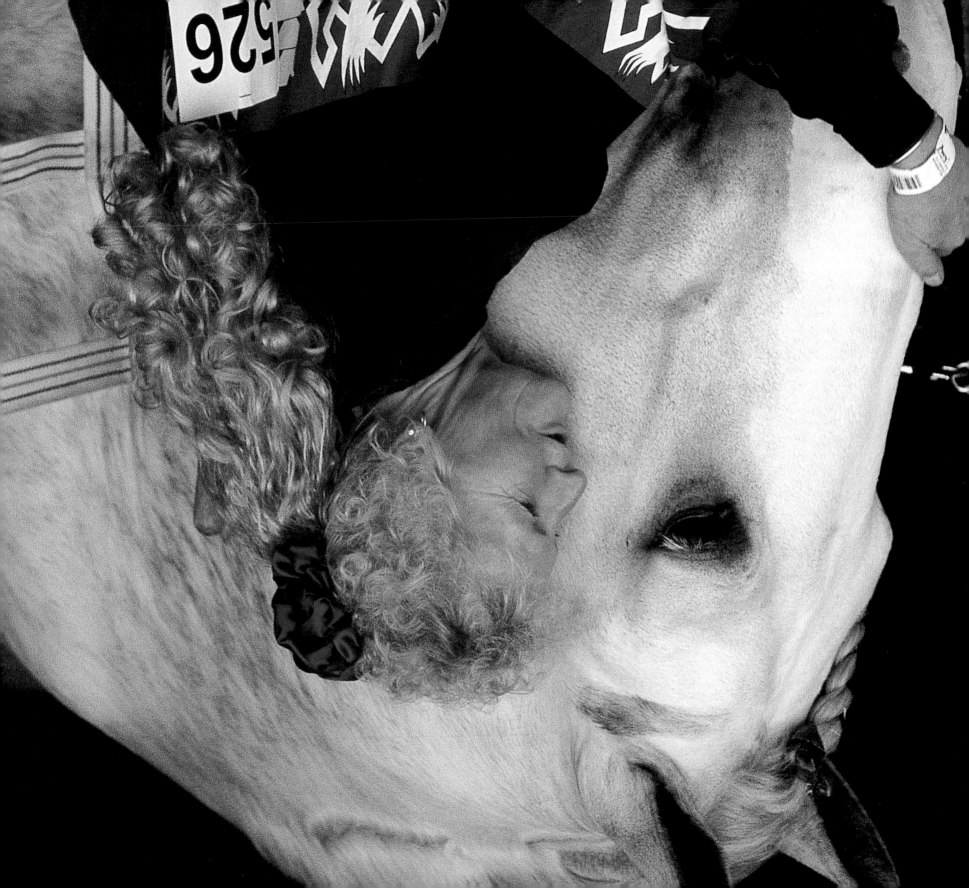

Not since dinosaurs roamed the planet has the earth shuddered with the step of a four-legged beast. Yet such can be the case when draft horses—called such because they've been selectively bred for their drafting, or pulling power—leave their stalls and march to their destination. At over 18 hands and 2,200 pounds, these heavy-duty workhorses are nearly the size of small elephants. Yet they have a rollicking swagger to their demeanor. Their walk is springy, their trot lofty and bold. And while their ancestors carried armored knights into battle with unwavering courage eons ago, today they are docile, tractable animals with eyes soft like liquid chocolate.

There is nothing that prevents modern draft horses from being ridden other than their backs are as broad as picnic tables and the notion of their massive weight being mastered by a few ounces of steel bit in their mouths elicits guffaws from most horse people. Yet, they are rideable. At most county fairs, where draft horse classes are standard entertainment for the horse show crowd, the bareback class for draft horses always draws a large group of spectators. The secret is that riding on most draft horses, thanks to their wide back and supple joints, is as comfortable as floating atop a mattress on a calm sea. It only looks like an awesome feat.

The draft horse is most at home in harness. When a workhorse is put in the traces and the driver holds the reins (called lines when driving), the gentle giant comes to life. *Stand aside*, he seems to say. *This is where I shine.* Whether hitched to cart or wagon or harrow, the draft horse serenades the senses of anyone enamored of horses. It is a symphony of percussion instruments: the clip-clop of the immense hooves reverberating like a drum, and the rhythmic jangling of the harness chains sounding like a tambourine.

Eric Scott and his wife Maribeth grow oats on 20 acres of farmland in central California. They set aside 8 acres each year that they manually work with their shire draft horses, an English breed of workhorse known for its tractable temperament. When I ask Eric why he refuses to surrender all of his land to the gas-powered tractor, Eric says unequivocally, "Once you work the soil with a horse and you've got your hands on the lines and you can feel the earth moving around your feet, you don't really have much interest in getting back on a mechanical tractor."

Opposite: English shire draft horse, Crys, has a head bigger than rider Maribeth Scott's entire torso. Above: Maribeth and Crys compete regularly.

41

A tall man, Eric explains that although he rode ranch horses for much of his life, "I was drawn to draft horses because I wanted a riding horse that was substantial." When he laid eyes on his first English-bred shire, a magnificent dappled silver stallion, he was smitten. Seven years ago, he bought his first shire filly. Now he and Maribeth own four of the gray horses. In fact, her pride and joy is a five-year-old stallion who was a combination birthday and Christmas gift from Eric. True to his heritage, the nearly alabaster stallion seems regal enough to carry his registered name of Illusion Crystal Clear of Oxkill. Yet he nuzzles the palms and shoulders of admiring onlookers with the blue-collar gusto befitting his nickname, Crys. "I've had all kinds of horses over the last 35 years," gushes an adoring Maribeth. "And this is the best horse I've ever owned." She is a petite woman, and quickly points out that Crys's head "is the size of my torso. So yes, I've taught him to respect me, but if he didn't have a kind heart and a great temperament, he could easily overwhelm me." For Maribeth, it's a love affair with her horse. She admits that horses have been a lifelong passion. "When I was five years old, I announced to my parents that I wanted a motorcycle. Instead, my dad decided he'd fix that, so he took me out to a riding stable and put me on a horse from the rental string. Well, that did it. I was hooked on horses. I can't tell you how many times my mother told my father, 'We should've gotten her the motorcycle.'"

While there are many different breeds of draft horses, each one hailing from a particular region or sporting a dominant color, the enthusiasm for those who love these workhorses doesn't waver. Those humans who choose to share their lives with these genial giants consider themselves fortunate.

One of those people is Roman Raber. He is the typical Midwestern farm boy–tall, strong, fit, and possessed of an easy smile. He is soft-spoken, the tone of his voice as level as that of an Iowa cornfield. Polite almost to a fault,

the only words he seems to utter without much contemplation are "Yes, Ma'am." Roman is the perfect complement to the Clydesdale draft horses he works with. He stands amid a trio of Clydesdales, placing one of his broad hands upon the brawny haunch of a bay gelding. "This is the best job in the world," he says, with one of those all-American smiles that guarantee he's telling the truth.

Roman is a driver for the team of Budweiser Clydesdales based in San Diego, California. He spends six months a year on the road with the team of 10 horses, traveling a mostly

Opposite: The Scotts own four gray shire draft horses. Above: Crys takes a breather before competing.

regional circuit on the West Coast that extends to points as far east as state fairs in Texas. The Budweiser Clydesdales are so famous and draw such a crowd at their exhibitions that Roman and his coworkers begin their day at 7:00 A.M. feeding, bathing, and grooming the horses, which includes braiding ribbons into their manes and tails. That way the horses are always ready to be admired by their fans.

The three Clydesdales tethered to the wash rack don't seem to mind the attention. Roman scrapes the bath water off their coats, and pats each one lovingly. He introduces the horses, who surround him like a stand of sequoias. "This is Pat and this is Earl and here's D.J.," he says. He identifies the two lead horses. Pat is a veteran at eight years old. D.J. is the youngster at four, but he already embraces his job like a trouper. "Believe me, they know when it's show time." Roman explains how after a few road trips, the newer trainees pick up on the routine: being fed, bathed, groomed, braided, and, finally, harnessed. Magically, there's a transformation in how the horses carry themselves. "They really begin to pick up their feet and arch their necks."

When pressed for which horse has endeared himself most to Roman, he shies away from the answer. Indeed, he is much like a father who can't name a favorite among his offspring. "I know them all individually, and they all have their own personalities, so I can't pick a favorite." Roman could be the Midwest's ambassador of equine diplomacy.

When I ask Roman how he ended up having "the best job in the world," he begins by explaining that he grew up on a farm in Iowa, where his family raised and trained draft horses. As the horses matured, they were taught the basics of farm work such as driving, and some of the stock was fitted for the show ring. "I basically grew up around horses," Roman says. He recalls a rite of passage, when he was taught to drive a team of draft horses. "When I was, oh,

about six years old, my dad just set me up in the driver's seat, handed me the lines, and said, 'Here you go.'"

Though his family primarily raised Belgians, the portly, mostly blond chestnuts of the workhorse world, Roman admits he's more smitten with the flashy Clydesdales. Who can blame him? Each one of the team is a bay of cherry red with an ebony mane and tail, a sweet white face, and a quartet of fluffy white stockings. The long white hairs on the fetlocks, called feathers, only add to the breed's appeal. Clydesdales sashay with every step, accentuating the proud cadence of the their trademark high-stepping trot.

"Personally, I love the Clydesdales," Roman says, a note of pride sneaking into his voice. "They're so pretty when you hitch up eight of them. There's not a prettier sight. You know, I work with them every day, and yet when we get all of them hitched up, and I see them go down the road, I still just think, 'wow!'"

Opposite: Roman Raber begins his day at 7:00 A.M. to prep the world-famous Budweiser Clydesdales. Above: Crys was a gift to Maribeth from her husband.

My Afternoon
with Wilma

I wasn't certain what I'd make of Wilma Tate. She is a local legend among the all-around riders, those equestrians who ride a little western, try a little English jumping, toss a rope around the neck of a calf. In 1985, she was inducted into the National Cowgirl Museum and Hall of Fame, in Fort Worth, Texas. Wilma Tate is enshrined right there alongside the likes of artist Georgia O'Keefe and movie legend Dale Evans.

When I drive up to her tidy, Spartan home in a dusty nowhere outside Hemet, California, I feel some trepidation. I am half afraid I'll be greeted at the door by an aged rodeo queen wearing clip-on crystal earrings, who might rant at me about how real riding has been sacrificed in the pursuit of winning ribbons in the show ring. I am, however, delightfully surprised.

At 79, Wilma Gunn Standard Tate is still spry and chatty, although she is a bit slowed by her eighth hip replacement surgery. She walks clutching a shiny wooden cane for support, but that doesn't deter her from accentuating her comments with a wave of her other hand. When I ask her how she could have eight hip replacements when she has only two hips, she says, "We've replaced one six

Opposite: Wilma Tate was a fixture on the 1950s rodeo circuit as a member of the color guard.
Left: Wilma's speciality was Roman riding.

49

times. My doctor finally told me, 'That's it. You've got to stop wearing them out. That's why I can't ride anymore. I can't take the risk.'

She begins her tale of a life spent on horseback with a recollection of her childhood. She grew up on a cotton farm outside of Lubbock, Texas. Her father would take her out to work the fields with him each morning, plopping tiny Wilma upon the broad back of one of the work horses. "I was just a little bitty thing. I remember just hanging onto the horse's mane."

When her parents divorced, Wilma moved to a Los Angeles suburb with her mother. Around age 12, she discovered the western lifestyle of horses, cowboys, and roping. There was a local Los Angeles county arena where wranglers met several times a week to practice roping and challenge each other for bragging rights. Having grown up on a cotton farm, Wilma had never seen a cowboy at work, nor had she experienced the thrills of calf roping. "I just thought calf roping looked like the greatest thing," She recalls thinking to herself. "Now that's what I want to do."

Within a few years, Wilma learned to rope, practicing by lassoing overturned buckets. She bought her first horse, a small, nondescript bay gelding she named Sonny. Even now when she says the horse's name there's a hint of nostalgia in her voice. "I did everything with that horse," she says rather wistfully. She clicks off his attributes. "He was fast and intelligent and smart and he loved to work." Unfortunately, Wilma's first outing with Sonny was disastrous. "The first calf I ever roped was off of Sonny. I reached down for my slack, but instead of grabbing the rope I grabbed my rein by mistake and jerked the horse around. I fell off, went under him, and he stepped on my face. The result was a jaw broken in four places.

Despite having her jaw wired together for six weeks, spunky Wilma continued to ride. Her family and non-horse friends thought she was a tad misguided in her passion. "Oh, I was always doing something crazy with horses," she laughs, shaking her head at the thoughts of her disdainful relatives.

By the 1950s, Wilma had become a fixture on the rodeo circuit. Sometimes she and two of her girlfriends traveled together. They were the color guard, carrying the stars and stripes around the arena on horseback after the bareback contests. Wilma, though, was known for her solo tricks on horseback. Her specialty was Roman riding, where two to four horses galloped abreast, while Wilma rode them by standing upright, balancing on the backs of two of the horses, a foot nestled upon each of their rippling spines. She had an entire routine that revolved around her uncanny ability to stay atop the team of horses. They even jumped small obstacles. The success of the act depended, though, upon her relationship with her beloved Sonny.

During one particular performance at a Tulsa, Oklahoma, rodeo, Sonny decided he wanted to upstage the queen of the cowgirls. After her Roman riding performance with four horses, Wilma worked toward the finale of the act. "I released the two center horses, then I went around with the two outside horses, one foot on the back of each, and I took them over the jumps. Then I dropped down onto Sonny's back and turned loose the third horse. Sonny was supposed to kneel and bow, and then get up and we'd back out of the arena. But this time, Sonny just ducked out from under me and took off."

Wilma landed on her feet. But this left her horseless in the center of the huge arena before a packed crowd, while her defiant horse careened around like a wild mustang enjoying his freedom. Eventually, Sonny came to a

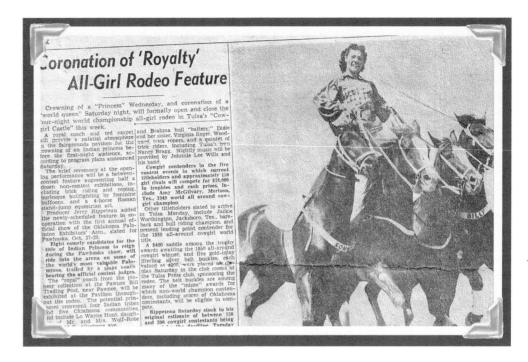

stop. He must've known how much trouble he was in because he strutted up to Wilma, his neck stretched out, and his head lowered in a submissive, almost apologetic stance. Over her shoulder, Wilma could hear the announcer say, "Well, folks, I don't know what she's up to now, but she's got something up her sleeve."

Wilma looked into the mischievous eyes of her horse. "He knew he'd done wrong," she says, laughing at the memory. "I told him, 'Thank God you came up to me. Now please, Sonny, don't let me down.' I knew I didn't dare make a grab for him, so I just cued him to bow, which he did." Then she asked him to lie down. He complied. Wilma kneeled and crawled across the bay horse's neck and sat upon his back. He turned his head to stare at her in that disarming way a horse has when he looks at his owner in such times. "Oh, you're such a bad boy," Wilma cooed to him

Opposite and above: Wilma and Sonny's show ring theatrics packed in the crowds and garnered headlines.

"As a young girl, I set this goal for myself to be a well-respected horseman, a true horseman."

— WILMA TATE

back then, "but I love you anyway." Then the two rose and took another bow. Right on signal, Sonny backed out of the arena with a flourish to end his impromptu performance.

Wilma's story is engaging. When I ask if she has a photo album of her escapades, she winks at me and begins to rise. I help her out of her chair and she ambles into another room and returns, cradling a hefty book.

When we sit again at the table, she pats the cover of the photo album, as if to pay it some sort of reverence, before opening to the first page. Then she opens the book as if she were lifting the lid of a treasure chest. The vintage black-and-white photos are captivating. I can almost hear the crackle of the arena loudspeaker, the snapping of the flag in the breeze, the whoops and applause of the crowds. In the pictures, Wilma is, of course, much younger: thick, curled hair (deep auburn, I guessed) with a pert nose, and a creamy complexion smooth as butter. But as she flips through the pages, she herself becomes transformed. Her voice becomes clearer, her granite-colored eyes sparkle, her speckled and weathered hands soften as she turns page after page of photos. On one page, she is a trick rider. On another page, she and one of her girlfriends, both of them outfitted in rodeo gear, pose atop the gate of a bucking chute for *The Saturday Evening Post*. True to the image of women in that era, she recalls the photographer had instructed the two cowgirls to "act like you're putting on lipstick." So they mock the action for the photograph. As she is telling the story, Wilma leans over to me and says in a whisper, as if she were telling me a secret that might destroy an illusion, "Notice I just hooked my horse's reins over the toe of my boot while I was doing it."

Time moved on for Wilma, in and out of the ring, marked by the advent of color photos in her album.

Sonny disappeared from the treasured archives, replaced by Appaloosas, palominos, and dappled grays. She knows the names and accomplishments of each horse, and mentions their gifts and shortcomings as a parent appraises her children. A brochure for *Wilma Tate's Riding School,* which she ran for 15 years, was tucked inside a sleeve of plastic. She holds that page fondly for a moment as if holding the hand of an old friend. I take that moment to ask her, "What has been your biggest reward for all the time you've spent with horses?" She looks up at me with eyes dewy with nostalgia and says without hesitation, "As a young girl, I set this goal for myself to be a well-respected horseman, a true horseman." Dismissing any reservations I had when I first pulled into her dusty driveway, I tell her she's certainly achieved her goal. "Yup," Wilma says, her face suddenly flush with a glow of pride, "if it was done on a horse, I did it."

Opposite: Wilma is now in the National Cowgirl Museum and Hall of Fame.
Above: The recipient of eight hip replacements, Wilma suffered her share of injuries in her heyday as a trick rider.

chapter
6

JOY

"*I loved horses, but the first time I actually rode was when I was 38.*"

– JOY RITTENHOUSE

You must look closely to notice that Joy Rittenhouse still walks with a slight unevenness to her step. Such a subtle variance cannot be called a limp. Yet it is there. Spend some time with her, though, and you're more absorbed with her petite blond features and her calm, self-assured way of speaking as she describes how she expresses her passion for horses. "I did not ride as a child," Joy explains, and then matter-of-factly reveals, "I had polio as a child. I had an atrophied right leg."

She grew up undeniably spunky, a trait she still exudes today. "I was always competitive and athletic, but I always had to contend with my leg. I loved horses, but the first time I actually rode was when I was 38." The New Jersey native had relocated to California and was on a vacation retreat when she got up the gumption to go on a trail ride. Despite some initial trepidation, she not only enjoyed the experience but also felt motivated to pursue riding more aggressively. That notion led to hunt-seat riding lessons and the purchase of her first horse, a gentle mare named Tina. "When I was on Tina, my leg wasn't a problem because she knew her job and did the work."

Not only did Joy's love of riding grow, but her leg became stronger, too. She began to realize that if riding made such a difference in her physically and emotionally—as it improved her self-esteem and feelings of accomplishment—perhaps she could share the same revelations with others who were struggling with some form of disability. Joy developed a plan of action that included educating herself about therapeutic riding programs through the North American Riding for the Handicapped Association (NARHA), participating in a one-year internship at the internationally known Fran Joswick Therapeutic Riding Center, and competing at nationally sanctioned horse shows in dressage and hunters. She received her teaching certification from NARHA in 1995 and currently operates an innovative

program called MACH 1, an acronym for Move a Child Higher, in Los Angeles, California.

One misconception Joy hopes to dispel is that therapeutic riding programs are mere pony rides for disabled children. In fact, the movement of the horse as he walks simulates the same basic movement humans display at a walk. Thus a rider with a physical disability such as cerebral palsy benefits from riding because her innate sense of balance compels her to stay in rhythm with the horse's gait. Pelvic, abdominal, and back muscles get strengthened, and posture improves. "If you're

Opposite: Having suffered from polio as a child, Joy Rittenhouse knows the benefits of therapeutic riding. Above: MACH 1 side walkers help a child learn to ride.

always in a wheelchair and always being carried, you have no way to develop those muscles," Joy says.

"We have a seven-year-old boy named Sam who's a student here. He got Most Improved at our horse show recently. When he first came to us—he has cerebral palsy—he couldn't sit up at all unassisted, even in a chair. I told his mom that maybe we'd give this a six-month trial period. I had him lie down, facing backward, resting his head on the horse's haunches, with his arms stretched out hanging over the horse's barrel [rib cage]. Well, Sam is now sitting up in a forward position in a little saddle with minimal assistance."

Joy's program has other success stories. She's devised interactive horseback games for the children, and those with disabilities such as Down syndrome and mild autism respond as well.

For example, in a game called pick a pocket, riders on horseback draw an instructional card from a colorful coin purse, and then follow the directions to perform simple tasks. Jonathon, a six-year-old with Down syndrome, seemed to delight in another game, lord of the rings, where he is asked to place colored plastic rings onto a narrow upright plastic pole. His mother watches approvingly from the sidelines and explains that her son can be difficult and is not one for following directions unless he's enjoying what he's doing. "But here he's very happy. He loves to ride. The activity stimulates his brain, and the riding improves his low muscle tone," Joey's mother says.

Joy's program couldn't function without her contingent of dedicated volunteers. Most often they work in a trio: one leads the horse while the other two are side walkers, placing a steadying hand on the rider for reassurance. But the horses are vitally important, too. And not just any horse can be indoctrinated into MACH 1. "Everyone wants to donate their wonderful, broken-down horse that is 23 years old," she says, acknowledging that it's understandable if horse owners desire an honored retirement for a loyal horse. But there are important criteria for a horse to qualify for MACH 1, most important is his ease and fluidity of motion. Since the primary benefit to disabled riders is through experiencing the healing rhythm of the horse's movement, Joy remarks, "When we look at a potential therapy mount, we evaluate its movement so we can see if it will be good for our clients."

A horse's temperament is also a point of evaluation for MACH 1. The horse must be willing to tolerate unintentional bumps from a rider's legs and unintentional tugs on the reins. And he cannot become bored with an hour or two of tedium at the walk. To remedy that, Joy sees that each mount is exercised regularly by an experienced rider and also has her recreation time in a paddock. Yet there are some horses who just never get with the program. One particularly memorable flunky was a Norwegian fjord. True to the breed's heritage as a small draft horse, the dun-colored gelding had previously worked as a driving horse, pulling carts and wagons. Apparently that occupation was still on his mind because, among other naughty tricks, he decided he'd had enough of the cross ties and began pulling his way back to his stall. He dragged the cross ties with him. "He now enjoys life in the state of Colorado," Joy says, laughing at his brief stay in Los Angeles. "And he's doing something other than being a therapeutic horse."

Currently the three treasured mounts at MACH 1 are Wrigley, Heidi, and Dr. Dotz. Wrigley is a Haflinger, which is a breed of small horses who originated in the Swiss Alps. The chestnut and flaxen gelding is the smallest of the three horses

and is often used for the smallest children. Heidi is a nice, well-mannered, obedient Norwegian fjord. At fifteen years old, the broad-backed mare's only fault seems to be that she and the handsome Wrigley engage in a love fest during rest periods, occasionally nuzzling and exchanging soft whinnies. The stout black-and-white pinto is Dr. Dotz. A former pack-horse, he was also once a lesson horse for beginners. The three horses are fat, sleek, and content. By their docile yet self-assured expressions it's not far-fetched to imagine they realize they're providing a noble service to their riders.

Just as Joy discovered that being on the back of a horse allowed her to compete against her peers with equality, she hopes that her students will also gain a sense of self-accomplishment. When one young girl, enthused with her session on horseback, broadly smiles and raises her hands above her head and claps, applauding herself, there is no doubt that Joy is accomplishing her goals, one child at a time.

Opposite: MACH 1 participants enjoy therapeutic rides and games.
Above: Joy and her faithful volunteers.

THE VIEW FROM THE BACK OF A HORSE

For some equestrians, the passion they feel for horses is life-giving. In the autumn of 1999, I was sitting atop my hunter at the back gate of a championship horse show awaiting my round. I remember reaching up and fingering the catheter that was implanted in my chest, just to reassure myself that it was still in place after a dozen practice jumps. I was battling a stubborn bone infection that kept sending me into the operating room, and the catheter was the port for monthly infusions of protective antibodies. Confident my medical apparatus was secure, I let the concern fade. I had a course of jumps to ride.

I wasn't the only rider defying doctor's orders that afternoon. I was aware that two of my fellow adult amateur competitors were also battling potentially devastating illnesses. One was undergoing kidney dialysis twice a week. The other, a young woman in her 20s, was sporting a pacemaker for her heart. We were quite the trio. But despite the potential calamities, we rode because that oneness with the horse, that power and spirit that exuded from the animals, seemed to infuse us with strength. We were riding almost with a vengeance, daring those forces from the dark side to pluck us from our saddles.

I met another brave soul mate on horseback the next year, Kathy Havens. I crossed paths with her in early 2000 on an Internet equestrian bulletin board. I was taken by her earthy humor and her incredible knowledge of horses. I contacted her personally and discovered she lived in Yuma, Arizona, not that distant from me. If two people could become fast friends via telephone and e-mail, it was Kathy and me.

I learned a lot about Kathy as our friendship grew. She had ridden much of her life and was a successful show competitor; then she survived an era as the owner of a dastardly horse who nearly ruined her confidence and was a source of constant frustration. No matter how much she babied him, introducing new skills patiently, he resisted the life of a competitive show horse and would intermittently burst forth into temper tantrums.

Kathy related the story of how she found her equine savior when she came upon a young Thoroughbred named Bud. "I traded the horse from hell for Bud," she told me. Bud's youth, however, gave her reservations. "He was only a three-year-old, so I was sure that this was going in the wrong direction."

When her trainer inspected Bud, she pronounced with a touch of disdain, "Bud is dull."

"But dull is good!" Kathy remarked, figuring a low-energy horse was an improvement over the high-octane one she currently owned. "His mind was so good, I figured if he was never more than a trail horse he'd at least allow me to enjoy riding again."

Bud not only did that, he won Kathy's heart. The scrawny young horse with the pencil-thin neck blossomed into a stout, beautiful chestnut gelding with a talent for dressage. We shared some of his progress notes. "He's like a worker bee," she told me, "a real tryer [sic]."

Then, in November, 2001, she informed me that she had been diagnosed with cancer. It was nearly hopeless, though Kathy would never use those words. Instead, she made jokes about ingesting a barium milkshake for her CT scan and the wonders of her new chemotherapy drug that didn't make her nauseous. Ever the faithful, passionate equestrian, Kathy continued to ride Bud. She sent me a photograph of her aboard her beloved horse, her oxygen tank housed in a backpack and strapped to her spine. She was smiling with all the gusto of a warrior who, if not winning the battle, was at least holding the front line. She attached a little note that said, "I forgot to tell you that a couple of years ago we decided that Bud's show name would be Life is Good. Kind of fitting now, huh?"

In March 2002, I was assigned to cover the United States Dressage Freestyle Championship in Los Angeles for both *Horse Illustrated* magazine and Horsecity.com, and it happened that Kathy was venturing out to watch with her friends. We decided to meet up at the competition. It wasn't hard to spot each other. I was wearing a clunky press pass around my neck and had a tape recorder stuck in my back pocket. Kathy was the nearly bald, painfully thin woman with an oxygen tank, wheezing with every breath. Yet still she greeted me with a laugh and the flip remark, "So, how did you recognize me?"

We sat together in the grandstand to catch up and watch the competition. I told her a few inside snippets about what was going on back at the barns with the Olympic-level riders. She enjoyed hearing the inside scoop. When I self-consciously lowered my voice and asked how she was doing, she reassured me with a disarming smile and revealed how, when her oncologist had given her the grim news that her cancer was terminal, she'd slapped her fist on the exam table and exclaimed, "But I just bought a brand new horse trailer!" I looked into her eyes and found myself pondering, "How can such a spirit ever be extinguished? How could her body fail her so?"

She seemed to sense my disbelief, and I'll always remember her efforts at being philosophical. "You know, Cindy, I realize I no longer have control over tomorrow. But I can control the transitions and gaits of my horse. I can control the responses of an entity who wants to work with me. The view from up there, on the back of my horse, is fantastic. When I'm up there, I'm not sick."

In mid-April, just as most riders are planning for horse shows and trail rides, Kathy passed away. I cried uncontrollably for a while, regretting the passing of someone who'd seemed so vibrant, so passionate about life and horses. At the very next horse show I competed in, I rode one round

just for her. I began my opening circle and headed to the first jump and thought silently to myself, "This one's for you, Kathy." I was having a most glorious performance on my young mare, perhaps even a winning round. But then at the last line of jumps, my horse misjudged the takeoff spot and bobbled the attempt, costing us first place. I could only laugh. I sensed Kathy sitting on the top row of the grandstand, clothed in riding breeches, a T-shirt, and a sun visor, shrugging her shoulders and giving me a knowing smile. *Horses. What are you going to do with them?*

Kathy Havens taught me lessons about horses and life that will remain with me forever. First, be patient. That dream horse will come along someday. Second, keep your sense of humor. It's a necessary component when dealing with both equines and adversity. But most of all, she taught me that the view from the back of a horse is indeed the best medicine for the soul.

Previous: Kathy Havens did not let cancer keep her from riding Bud, even when she had to strap an oxygen tank to her back.

chapter
8

BRONZED
BEAUTIES

"*I'm always able to come up with something new.*"

– LISA GORDON

oesn't every horse-crazy kid first express his or her love for horses in some form of artwork? While other children are dutifully drawing stick figures of the human nuclear family, the horse-obsessed youngster puts crayon to paper and creates an entire panorama of wild horses with flowing manes cavorting in fields of grass and daisies. There are no human forms present on that canvas.

I was no different as a child. Assigned to sketch a likeness of my family in third grade, I recall being chastised for my creation. Though my parents were indiscernible from hors d'oeuvres on toothpicks, the token horse—a pure figment of my imaginary home life—was blessed with a cascading mane, detailed knee and hock joints, a decidedly Arabianesque face, and pink, flaring nostrils. As always, he was embodied in an ebony coat, with a mane and tail the color of snow. He was my dream horse, and for years he made his appearance in my artwork. Perhaps I felt that if I drew him, eventually that very horse, in the flesh, would arrive on my doorstep. It wasn't until much later I realized that no such color combination—the black horse and the white mane and tail—existed naturally in the equine world. But a young girl with a box of crayons can still dream.

One horse-crazy young girl who grew into a full-fledged equestrian artist is Lisa Gordon, a resident of Santa Fe, New Mexico. She has nurtured a reputation for combining the graceful, almost sensuous, figure of the horse with geometric forms such as spheres, cubes, and rectangles. Her medium is bronze sculpture and her themes are universal; they resonate with horse lovers who readily accept the horse as a suitable metaphor for some of life's most momentous experiences. For example, her bronze piece *Straight and Narrow* is a presentation of an upper level dressage horse in an extended trot as he stretches from one pillar to another suspended between the two points by a narrow beam of bronze. With one hind hoof just leaving where it had recently trod, and one front hoof touching down at a new beginning, the sculpture conveys the eternal struggle to remain on the straight and narrow as we venture from one station in life to another. With all the concentration of a gymnast on a balance beam, the dressage horse maintains her focus to stay on the chosen path. The sculpture is just one of the many ideas Lisa brings to fruition in bold relief.

"I'm always able to come up with something new," Lisa says from her Santa Fe studio. She reflects on how her childhood love of horses led her to express that devotion in bronze sculptures. "From day one I was always a horse-crazy girl. I drew horses, played horses, collected the Breyer model horses, you name it. I was a shy, reclusive little girl, and I think eventually my parents thought if they

Opposite: Lisa Gordon's passion for horses manifested in the form of a sculpting business. Left: Lisa's first pony had two speeds—fast and faster.

Lisa owned two quarter horses after Daisy, Playmate and Hobbie. They both were primarily pleasure mounts, but with her aunt being a professional trainer, Lisa soon found herself schooling her horses for the show ring. She wasn't a dedicated, avid competitor, but she enjoyed working with her horses herself. "The most rewarding part of owning and working with my own horses was the intimate dialogue I could develop if I listened hard enough."

A need to express that age-old mystical bond between horse and human is what helped lead Lisa to an art major in college. At first, though, not everyone was thrilled with her decision. "When I went to college, around my second year, I announced that I wanted to be an art major. I know my parents thought, 'Oh geez, we just threw away our money, but at least she'll earn a degree in *something*.' I had originally considered being something like a professional photographer, taking pictures at horse shows. But then I happened to take a class in bronze casting and foundry work." That entire creative process appealed to her. Lisa knew she had to be a sculptor.

Both Lisa and her parents were encouraged by the critique of a professor, her mentor, who praised her talents during one of her student shows. "His words were something like, 'Nicely sculpted horse. But now what are you going to do with it? There are hundreds of people who can sculpt a horse, but what are you going to do that's different with this historical figure?' I knew I didn't want to do purely anatomical studies," she says. So she began to explore various themes that allowed her to use the horse as a metaphorical figure for her personal life experiences.

Within her body of work there are two paths of expression: the collection of childhood reflections that portray images such as a young girl playing with horses, and

Above: Some of Lisa's sculptures are created for corporate offices.

bought me a horse it'd bring me out of my shell. It did give me more self-confidence."

The confidence builder came in the guise of Daisy, a scruffy pony bestowed upon Lisa when she was 13 years old. "Daisy had a reputation throughout the county," Lisa recalls. "Daisy had two speeds: fast and faster," she laughs. "Plus, she was an escape artist. Her nickname was Houdini because she quickly learned how to let herself out of any stall or corral." Lisa wasn't the first little girl to own the Welsh-cross pony with the flaxen mane and tail, and she wouldn't be the last.

ones conveying more adult themes such as a piece entitled *Career Moves*. Both are wrought with personal touches.

Her bronzes are offered at several galleries in the United States. When a gallery hosts a show featuring her work, she incorporates a theme, whether it's one of whimsy or one that is more reflective. "I am not sure what people feel when they are with my art," Lisa says, contemplating how her bronzes affect the observer. "Not everyone is horse-crazy. Many of my clients are not horse people, either. However," she says, reflecting on the undeniable appeal of the horse, "the horse is an image in which people can identify. Horses represent freedom, power, and conquest all in one package. I think they're a subliminal metaphor for those ideals."

Lisa acknowledges that since early people first scrawled images of wild horses on their cave walls with sticks of charcoal, horses have been a part of our artistic history. "Possibly the horse is a link to our past. And the art, the way I present the horse, is a real link to our present. It makes for an interesting dichotomy."

The consummate artist, Lisa explains the differences between the four types and sizes of bronzes she creates. "The smaller works are called sketches. Though I offer about one dozen to thirty of each of these, they are individually sculpted, so each can't help but take on its own personality. Next are garden-size pieces, which are up to 5 feet tall." These might find a home in an atrium, courtyard, or upscale office or restaurant. "Maquettes are prototypes or smaller versions of an architectural piece. Some artists make them scale models, but mine are not. They're more a representation of what my larger piece will look like." Finally, the architectural bronzes are the largest sculptures. "They are designed for public display," she says, explaining that they'd be placed at a business or office complex, or perhaps in a large equestrian center.

For now, Lisa's stable of bronzes will have to keep her company, since Lisa doesn't own any horses. That's something she hopes to rectify in a short while. Asked if she at least rides, she sighs and relates that a part-time relationship with someone else's horse wouldn't satisfy her. She still longs for that close companionship she can find only with a horse she owns herself, one she can work with on a daily basis. Perhaps one of her sculptures is her talisman, her dream horse, which will once again gallop into her life.

Above: Until she gets a live horse, Lisa's stable of sculptures will keep her company.

IN ALL FAIRNESS

"*If I wanted to be a successful competitor, I wanted to learn about judging.*"

– Elizabeth Shatner

Anyone who regularly competes at horse shows ought to be blessed with a thick skin and a craving for melodrama. Nowhere else in the equestrian world is there such a contrast between pageantry and palpable nervous tension as when riders line up in the center of the show arena. It is there that they await their fate. As the loudspeaker crackles to attention, the final thought on the minds of participants is *Who did the judge think was the best?*

Only one rider can receive the blue ribbon, and the horse show judge has the unenviable task of deciding who leaves the arena gushing with pride and stroking his or her horse's neck, and who slinks back to the barn contemplating what went wrong. Sometimes riders and spectators lack insight into the hows and whys of ribbon placements. They blame the judge for being either politically motivated or blatantly blind. But in all fairness, the vast majority of horse show judges are above reproach. Lifelong horse lovers, they pursue stringent requirements such as attending judging clinics and passing exams to obtain their credentials. Competitors and trainers themselves, they know firsthand the challenges of competition and acknowledge the responsibilities that come with the job. Elizabeth Shatner is a perfect example of a fair and empathetic horse show judge.

She had her first experience with judging horses as a member of the Indiana State Arabian Youth Judging Team in the mid-1970s. "I felt like that was an important part of the horse business," she says, and explains her reasoning. "If I wanted to be a successful competitor, I wanted to learn about judging." By winning several junior judging competitions, Elizabeth was allowed to attend the Arabian judging clinics offered to adult officials. "I took it all quite seriously, and I've been at it ever since."

Currently she holds more than a half-dozen credentials for judging recognized shows, events that are sanc-

tioned by national breed or riding associations. As she lists the cards she holds—Arabian, National Show Horse, American saddlebred, saddle seat equitation, roadster, and hackney harness—she pauses and says with an enthused smile, "And the most recent one is for judging Andalusians, which are sort of my new favorite curiosity."

One can't ignore that Elizabeth is drawn to certain breeds that, as a group, boast lofty gaits, elegantly arched necks, and voluminous manes and tails. "Aesthetically I'm drawn to the romantic-type horse," she says, and instinctively draws a curvaceous, sweeping line in the air. The gesture mimics the swanlike necks and rounded toplines of horses with Arabian, saddlebred, and Andalusian blood. "I feel like a fairy princess when I'm riding a white Andalusian."

Yet when judging a show, she's forced to put her romantic visions aside. "It's my quest as a judge to recognize quality, and the breed type and standard, and how it

Opposite: Horse judge Elizabeth Shatner holds several judging credentials.
Left: Elizabeth says she is "a sucker for a cute pony."

Right: Elizabeth hopes that watching a competition will inspire a child to get involved with showing.

should be judged. I have absolutely no problem being objective. That's what I'm hired for." Outside of the parameters of the judge's booth, though, she lets the soul of a true horse lover express itself. "I have a great appreciation for any horse. Even a scruffy little horse with a kind look in its eye—I just love those types of horses." Then she adds quietly, almost as a secretive aside, "I'm a sucker for a cute pony."

That affinity for cute ponies arises from her first memories of wrestling with her uncle's pinto pony named, ironically, Lady. Born in Illinois, Elizabeth recalls her frustration while trying to coerce Lady into a trail ride down a country road. "I could only get her so far down the road away from the house before she'd do this sort of benign U-turn and head home. I must've been only six years old at the time," she says, laughing at the remembrance of her determination versus that of a defiant pony. "It was my first introduction to the world of horse training. I just worked and worked at it because I wanted so badly to get her past that spot in the road."

Fortunately, Elizabeth's next venture was with a more accommodating pony. When she was eight, her parents gave her Little Bit, a buckskin Galiceno. Though the odds were against her, being a little girl with a green, two-year-old pony, she has only fond memories. "I probably should've been killed, but that pony was just wonderful." When asked to describe Little Bit, Elizabeth uses the language of an astute horsewoman, but her affection for the small buckskin is evident. "She was only 56 inches tall, about 14 hands, but she was a mile long. Honestly, I could fit two friends behind me!" Not only did Elizabeth gain self-confidence on the pony, she learned the importance of recognizing the peculiarities of individual breeds. "When I got older, I wanted to show her in pet and pleasure pony classes so I had to teach her how to do a jog-trot. It took me forever! Later on, when I read up on Galicenos, [a rare breed of smooth-gaited Spanish ponies], I found out why: They are bred to have a running walk," a gait similar to America's Tennessee walker.

She says the horse show bug bit her early on. "For me, I originally was attracted to showing because I liked the challenge. I enjoyed spending all the time in the preparation, in making my horse beautiful. Plus it was great family time. My parents and I would load up the trailer and we'd go to the little local shows." While she's had years of exposure to the heady world of nationally ranked horse shows, where a proven champion can sell for six figures, she doesn't hesitate to mention her austere beginnings. "We were very grassroots. We did it on our own. The first show we went to we discovered, 'Oh, the horses have to back up in the lineup!' So there we were, my dad and I before the class, trying to teach the pony to back up."

From her early years on the back of a pony, Elizabeth went on to train a few horses privately for clients, then to teach students and run successful training stables in Kentucky, Michigan, and California alongside her late husband Mike Martin. Now married to actor William Shatner (an accomplished horseman in his own right), Elizabeth has regained her amateur status for competition purposes. The Shatners' stable includes champion saddlebreds and an impressive assortment of quarter horses trained for western-style reining competition. She comments that her return to amateur status will allow her to show in more events and also give her a more relaxed perspective. "Sometimes when you're competing as a professional, there's a certain amount of pressure on you to win in order to maintain your reputation. I think there can be a danger of losing sight of why you started showing in the first place, which is the love of the horse."

Her love for horses and for competing, plus her many years as a trainer and instructor, have held her in good stead as a judge. "I'm definitely more empathetic toward the exhibitor," she says, explaining how she has a habit of asking the steward to check the riders for proper attire and tack before they enter the arena. "We [judges] have to go by the rule book. So, for instance, if it says that a scarf or bolo tie is mandatory, I have to eliminate any riders who don't comply." When told she's a judge with a heart, she replies, "Well, I want to always encourage someone to compete and get through the class successfully and be judged against their peers. I never want to inhibit that."

This is not to imply that Elizabeth is a total softy. Her lanky, suntanned blond good looks belie the authoritative side

that helped make her a respected horse trainer. "While judging an amateur pleasure driving class at the 2002 Andalusian National Horse Show, I had a great save." She becomes animated as she recounts the near-tragedy. "This lady exhibitor was driving a two-wheeled cart when her horse began to buck. I don't know why, but these sorts of things always seem to happen right in front of me. Against what was probably my better common sense, I yelled out, 'Circle! Circle!' Then, as the horse came by me," she says, describing how the horse was nearly out of its harness and kicking toward the driver's chest, "I just reached up and grabbed a rein and yelled, 'Whoa!' in my best trainer's voice." She brought the naughty, rambunctious horse to a halt and got the proceedings under control.

Though she's still a much sought-after judge, Elizabeth has been earning plenty of her own blue ribbons and accolades. She had great praise for a leggy, feminine American saddlebred filly with the swanky moniker The Glitz. With Elizabeth riding, the dappled gray won the Western Pleasure championship at the 2002 St. Louis National Charity Horse Show. Astride the sleek filly during a recent schooling session, Elizabeth nearly looked the part of a fairy princess.

But it isn't necessarily all trophies and limelight that she hopes to convey to those new to the world of horses. "I always have a plan when it comes to kids and horses," she says. "I want to impart respect and understanding for the horse, including its role in our history and culture." She explains the potential of a child or adult spectator watching a reining class and becoming so intrigued by the maneuvers that he or she might come to realize the horse's contribution to ranching and the development of the west. Hopefully, then, that person can gain an appreciation for the horse as a dependable workmate and might also be inspired enough to climb upon the back of a scruffy little horse. You know the type: one with a kind look in his eye.

chapter

10

THE HORSE
OF A LIFETIME

If a rider has one horse in a lifetime who is so special that his memory causes eyes to mist, not with regret but with fond memories, many years after the animal's passing, then she is indeed a fortunate horse person. My girlfriend Pam and I are a couple of those lucky ones.

Though Pam Mahony now lives in Kentucky, she spent years competing in the amateur owner hunter classes at major English horse shows, much of the time on the West Coast. In fact, we were contemporaries. No doubt we passed each other at the back gate of venues such as Del Mar and Santa Barbara, but because we rode in separate age divisions we never really got acquainted. It was only years later that we began comparing notes and realized that, like the show hunters we rode, we had some things in common. We are passionate about horses. We've both ridden most of our lives and are now ignoring the creaks and aches as we climb into the saddle because, frankly, that's where we feel most at home. We also both collect horses. Our horses pepper our respective family ranches, springing up in pens and stalls, each one fresh and green and full of promise. And then we give them cute names as if they're our children. I've had Arthur, Vinnie, and Barbie. She's had Sophie, George, and Warren. But our closest connection comes from being part of a sort of private club in which the members reverently acknowledge that they were somehow chosen to know once-in-a-lifetime horses.

Pam's special horse was named Valor. To a horseman's trained eye, Valor had a sloping shoulder, a massive hip, and nice, straight legs. But Pam admits, "When I first saw Valor in Stillwater, Minnesota, he was an 11-year-old plain bay horse with about a dozen chunky braids in his mane. He was totally uninspiring to an amateur's eye." And yet Pam and her plain bay gelding began a string of championships that lasted five years. The horse loved to compete. "He understood when he was 'on,' " Pam recalls. "We invariably had bad warm-ups, but let him walk in the ring and he was a different horse."

As with all sports champions, Valor had his personality quirks. For example, he didn't enjoy being fussed over. He did not have a backyard pet mentality. What he did have, though, was a craving for citrus fruit. "Let him smell an orange and he'd run over you to get at it," Pam laughs. "Once at a horse show in Chagrin Falls, Ohio, I was leading Valor back to his stall. They had a fresh lemonade/limeade stand that he had to walk right by, and I was not paying attention. Well, Valor did a sharp right turn to the juice stand and almost climbed over and into it before I could catch him. He wanted those lemons and limes!" The experience taught Pam that to placate his cravings she needed to show up at his stall every morning with several oranges. "Otherwise he wouldn't talk to me all day."

My special horse was named Baba Yaga. I cannot recall his official registered name printed on his American quarter horse papers, but he was christened after I listened to a rendition of Mussorgsky's *Pictures at an Exhibition* and liked the heavy, brooding sound of the piece entitled "The Hut of Baba Yaga." The fact that in Russian folklore Baba Yaga is a female witch and my horse was a gelding didn't deter me.

Just like Valor, Baba Yaga was a rather plain bay with a rather plain head. Standing still, or relaxing in his stall, he wouldn't win any beauty contests. But get him into a gallop over a course of jumps and he would cruise like a big cat and jump like an antelope. Just like Valor, Baba Yaga was a champion who loved competing for a blue ribbon. If I got him in to a jump a little wrong, he'd pin his ears in frustration, then explode into a buck when his front feet hit the ground. It was as if he were punishing me for keeping him out of the winner's circle.

To be truthful to the past, the horse actually had belonged to my sister Jill. He was her baby, her pride and joy. They had years of success in the show ring before I inherited

Opposite: The author bonded with her sister's horse, Baba Yaga.

"Let him smell
an orange
and he'd run
over you to
get at it."
– PAM MAHONY

him, so I often felt a certain pressure to perform, as if I had no excuse for not being show champion. What heightened my performance anxiety was that Baba Yaga had the character of an impetuous clown. If show time festivities were too dull and boring, he'd create silly antics that amused both him and spectators, but infuriated me. He'd prance on tippy-toes or curl his upper lip to reveal his teeth, as if laughing at some hilarious inside joke. During flat classes, if the judge made us work too long at the trot, I would often feel him balling up under me like a coiled spring, threatening to unleash some acrobatics. He'd decided things weren't progressing quickly enough, his dinner was waiting, and it was time to move the contest along. I can remember times when I begged him under my breath to behave until the ribbons were decided. Sometimes he accommodated me.

While Valor had a thing for citrus, Baba Yaga was a big fan of sweets. His favorite treats at horse shows were cinnamon buns sold out of little pink food carts at the county fairs or fresh cotton candy. In a pinch, a donut would suffice. Once my sister and I were leading Baba Yaga to the back gate of the show ring past the entry booth when he spied a box of jelly donuts set out for the judge and volunteers. A 1,400-pound horse is an entity to be reckoned with, especially when he is drawn, zombielike, to a raspberry-filled glazed donut. His big gray lips flung the entire box off the table, sending humans, clipboards, and paper forms flying. He ended up with a donut handily inside his mouth.

Over the years, Baba Yaga became blind in one eye. But that never deterred his winning ways. I won the regional amateur adult hunt-seat medal finals on him in 1982, a feat even more incredible because at the final jump–a brick wall off a tight turn–the show photographer snapped a picture on the horse's sighted side, using a bright flash. The horse surely was blinded at the point of takeoff.

Baba Yaga lived to the age of 26, retiring on our ranch and first becoming a mount for our young cousins, then assuming the role of lawn ornament. We'd open his paddock gate and he'd stroll around our ranch, nibbling at grass and visiting with his neighbors. He never had a lavish send-off, but over the 23 years we knew him, he was part of our family. Jill and I think often of him, and fondly.

In contrast, Valor received grand honors at his retirement from the show ring. Pam explained that, "Three times he was champion amateur owner hunter at the Grand National Horse Show, at the Cow Palace, in San Francisco. My trainer, Linda Hough, had decreed all summer that Valor would be retired in 1984, after the Cow Palace. He was losing some step [length to his stride] and it was a little harder for him to make it down the lines. He was 17 years old. I knew Linda was right. We had to let him go out on top and not get beat by horses that were not as good. We owed it to him."

Pam's horse stepped from the limelight in fine fashion. She and Valor cruised to one of their trademark winning rounds in the stake class to earn the show's championship. Unbeknownst to Pam, her trainer had prepared a tribute to the horse. So while the championship ribbon and trophy were awarded to Pam and Valor, the show announcer read Valor's accolades. It couldn't have been a better tribute. "And there he goes," Pam says the announcer remarked as she led her horse from the arena, "Valor–a true champion leaving the ring for the last time." He spent his retirement years relaxing in a pasture with a pony and a miniature donkey as companions. Valor quietly passed away at 24.

Valor and Baba Yaga: two big plain bay geldings with so much in common. They were both honest, solid citizens in the horse show world. And they were both horses most riders dream about.

RIDES WELL
WITH OTHERS

There's something I find soothing about a solitary trail ride with a horse. There's no conversation to disturb the lullaby of saddle leather as it stretches with every stride of my horse. No silly banter to interrupt me as I contemplate the nature of the universe or which television show I'll watch that evening. And yet I've experienced undeniable fun on horseback when I've ridden as part of a group.

Though I consider myself an experienced, rather sophisticated technical rider, I can easily revert to a giddy cowgirl of sorts, letting my equitation lapse and my concerns for my horse's proper head carriage and tempo of gaits fall by the wayside. Just put me with a group of riders outside the constraints of a horse show arena and I'm likely to unleash my inner Annie Oakley. Similar to a kindergartner who is the diplomat of the sandbox, whose report card reads, "Plays well with others," it can be said of me that I ride well with others.

I've ridden in parades as part of a group. In horse shows I've been a member of hunt teams, a team made up of a quartet of matched horses who course over jumps. Many times I've cast aside my better judgment and accompanied skilled, yet secretly rambunctious, equestrians on trail rides that disintegrated

Opposite: Painted Magic, a female drill team, has performed at the Tournament of Roses Parade on several occasions. Left: A member of the Galloping Gossips works the crowd.

Above: Love of horses and friendship with like-minded horsewomen are the foundations for Painted Magic.

Magic, based in the horse community of Norco, California. The group was formally established in 1992, and the highly disciplined women aboard their colorful paint horses are well known throughout the southern California region. The drill team has ridden in the famed Tournament of Roses parade a half-dozen times, and they've performed at professional rodeos and equestrian competitions. They also find time to donate the proceeds of performances to charitable causes such as the Make-A-Wish Foundation, which grants wishes to desperately ill children, many of whom have a passionate desire to spend time with a beautiful horse.

Adele, an engaging woman who's astride her ebony-and-white spotted filly, describes the somewhat serendipitous beginnings of the group. "I was sitting up here [at the local rodeo grounds] on my old horse, a paint gelding named Mark, when this woman rode up to me on her paint and asked me if I wanted to join a drill team. I told her I'd definitely think about it, because just that morning I'd woken up and realized I didn't have any friends to ride with. Well, she told me where the team was going to practice on Tuesday night. Tuesday night came around, my husband called and said he was working late and wouldn't make it home for dinner, so I left him a note on the refrigerator and I was gone." A few incarnations later Painted Magic has become, in the words of Valentina, the president, "A cohesive unit based on the love of the horse and friendship with other horsewomen."

Though there are currently a dozen members, Valentina says the group could eventually use about 20 riders. But there are some criteria. "Our bylaws, and there are four pages of them, say you can't have any kicking horses," she says, which is understandable considering that in some routines the horses are literally nose to tail or haunch to haunch.

The group also requires a level of commitment and coexistence. "It's hard to keep a lot of women together,"

into galloping melees. But I've yet to experience being part of a drill team. Not only do they ride fast and attempt daredevil maneuvers, they also get to wear snazzy matching outfits. Sometimes they carry flags. Now that looks like fun!

Valentina Perrah and Adele McCandlish are two of the founding members of the all-female drill team Painted

Adele offers, "because they all have families. It becomes all about priorities. And then, of course, whenever you have a group of women together, there are the personality clashes that sometimes can't be avoided."

The horses seem to get along fine, though, even when the group's members do not. Some horses are so even-tempered and trustworthy that they perform bridleless, with nothing more than leather straps around their necks to guide them. "The horses learn the drills before the riders," Valentina explains. "We learn one routine at a time. It takes the rider about 90 days to learn the new routine, but the horse learns all the movements in about 30. They get to where they take their cues from the whistle," she says, referring to the team leader who blows a shrill whistle to signal a transition. And though the twice-weekly practices are done at a slow lope so that each stride, turn, and precision stop becomes instinctive, the real performances are choreographed for a full gallop. "They know when they're on stage," Valentina says. She points out one rangy handsome gelding with a long, wavy tail. "He's 15 years old. He's been doing this for 12 years. In fact," she says, "he was broke to drill. He started doing this as a 3-year-old."

About 100 miles east of Painted Magic territory is another female drill team. The Galloping Gossips is based out of the Imperial Valley area of California, near the Arizona border. The team of eight riders performs traditional square dance movements choreographed to suit skills on horseback. The team performs in parades, rodeos, charitable events, and as halftime entertainment at major horse shows. Since square dancing typically requires both male and female participants, half of the riders dress in long skirts and half wear chaps. When asked if there's any discourse over who gets to wear the dresses and who is assigned the batwing chaps, spokesperson Sherry O'Malley says that really isn't much of an issue, perhaps because of the personal dynamics of the group. "We're not a group with a flowing routine. We don't have this great finesse to our performances. We're all glitter and guts." And the division of labor between the female and the pseudo male riders is clearly defined. "The 'guys' do the maneuvering, the tighter turns; the 'girls' are in charge of setting the pace and maintaining proper spacing."

The Galloping Gossips was formed in 1957 primarily as a trail and pleasure riding activity for women. As the group evolved into its current form of dancing on horseback, its social atmosphere changed. The group's name originated from the postrehearsal activity of going out to lunch and sharing harmless local gossip around the table. What might have been idle chatter in the past has now become, in the words of Sherry, "cheap therapy." She says, "Every once in a while we'll have a gal join whose husband or significant other gets very jealous of our weekly nighttime practice sessions. It causes a lot of stress. We can see how this conflict really affects her. But by the end of that night's practice, after we've walked our horses around and talked while we cool them out, she's back to being relaxed and has a better perspective on life."

Just as their counterparts in Painted Magic, the Galloping Gossips constantly struggle with finding members who can truly dedicate themselves to a team. Sherry cites that struggle as the biggest challenge of keeping the unit intact. "Women today have so many demands on their time. There aren't just family issues, but often they have a job as well." Her biggest frustration is the member who'll come to all the practices, learn the dance routine, plan for a show, and then make only a tentative commitment. "That's the worst part, when at the last minute they say something like, 'I'll be there as long as something doesn't come up.' That's why we really try to get members who understand from the beginning that we depend on them."

"We just can't have any green horses. They must be seasoned, well-broke horses."

—Valentina Perrah, Adele McCandlish

They also depend on their horses. Sherry has two square dance mounts. One is Nevada, who is 27 years old and nearing retirement. The other is Chuck who, by comparison, is a youngster at 16. But the group's horses needn't necessarily be older models. "We just can't have any green horses. They must be seasoned, well-broke horses."

Unlike Painted Magic's spotted horses, horses in the Galloping Gossips can be of any color. "We do try to match the pairs, or somehow coordinate the colors of the horses. But it's not the most important thing." She does confess, however, to tinkering with nature at least once. "Oh, a number of years ago we happened to have all solid, dark-colored horses except for one paint. We were getting ready to ride in the Tournament of Roses parade and we thought it would just look so much better if all the horses matched. So yes," she giggles, "we dyed the white patches on the paint."

So there is a touch of girlish hijinks to go along with the gossiping, the guts, and the glitter. These drill teams do indeed sound like something I might have to investigate firsthand. I have a lovely palomino mare who enjoys the company of other horses and who doesn't mind learning new skills. And heaven knows the excitement and pageantry of drill teams appeal to me. Plus, I do ride well with others.

Opposite and left: Drill teams like Painted Magic and the Galloping Gossips require a sense of humor and commitment.

12

ON PARADE

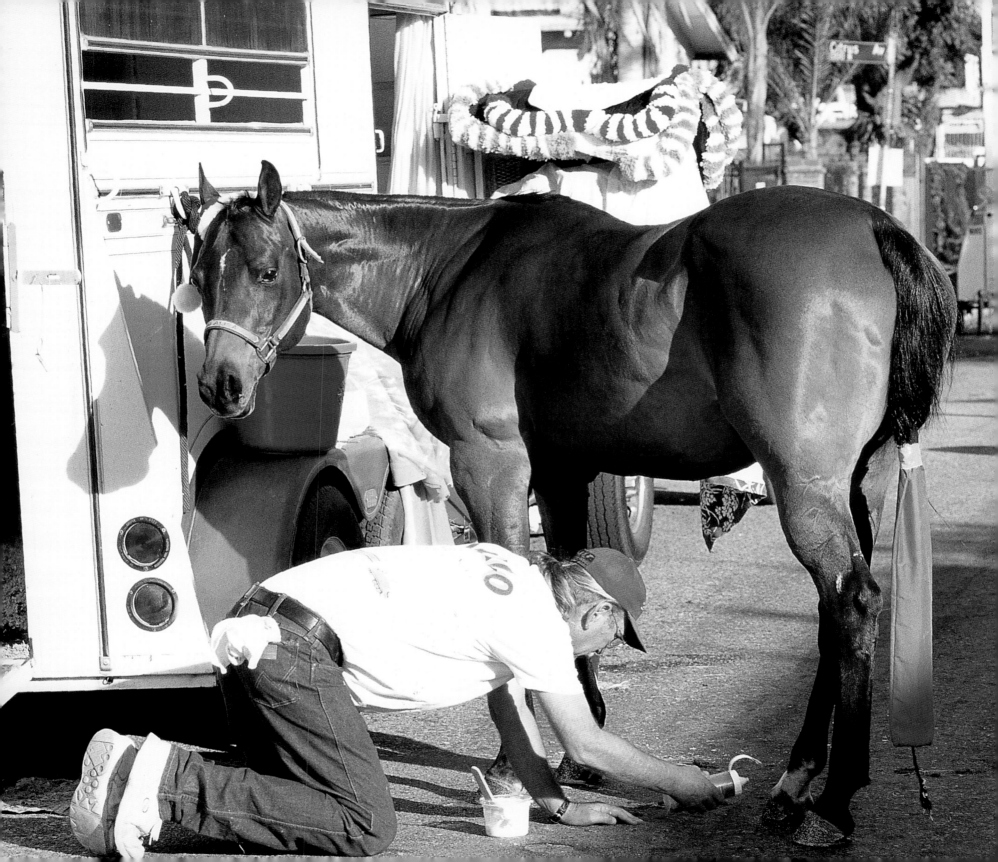

I t is a late afternoon at the start of the Christmas season in southern California. As the sun yawns and settles behind the San Gabriel Mountains, the temperature dips to 60 degrees, which is the seasonal cue for the natives to break out their cotton turtlenecks. Santa Claus is also stirring the conscience of the metropolis as Hollywood is gearing up for its 72nd Annual Christmas Lane Parade. Streets clogged with city busses, sports cars, taxicabs, and street vendors will soon become host to thousands of spectators who'll sit cross-legged on cement curbs or nestled in folding chairs. Since this is Hollywood, the parade will include an ensemble of television and movie stars riding the route in classic cars. And there will be the marching bands, serenading the onlookers with bass drum-enhanced carols. Yet what will draw the most attention, what will cause the city kids to jump from curbside or spring from their parent's knees, are the horses. Resplendent in sequins and sparkling in silver, horses and riders will soon strut downtown and woo the crowd.

Just before dark, a caravan of horse trailers chaperoned by traffic cops is led through the anxious crowd and parks on residential streets cordoned off by patrol cars. The horses line the quiet streets tethered to the sides of their trailers, their hind hooves sometimes resting on sidewalk cement and their mouths occasionally nibbling on shrubbery. The anticipation surely rivals that of Santa's elves on Christmas Eve.

In a flurry of activity, riders groom their horses to perfection and put a finishing touch of polish on their tack. Because it is a holiday parade, festive touches adorn the horses. Several tails sport poinsettia corsages. Tinsel is braided into the manes of a pair of pintos. A pretty bay mare stands silently to be primped. John Polak is her owner and rider. He paints her hooves with craft glue then

dusts them with a sprinkling of green glitter. A dedicated parade rider, he's traveled quite a distance to participate. He looks up from where he's crouched beside his mare's feet and remarks with a smile that the evening's venture will cost him $150 in gasoline. "But it's worth it to see the kids' faces."

Whether it's the holiday cheer or the excitement of preparing to dazzle the public, there isn't an unkind word spoken. What is evident is a love for horses and an enthusiasm for sharing it. Horse people love a parade.

Opposite: Most parade riders participate not for money, but for the joy of parading and making spectators happy.
Above: Even tails are decorated for the holidays.

Among the throng of equestrians, Kerry Walsh and her silvery white Arabian gelding can't help but command attention. Snuggled into her slinky costume bejeweled with sequin paisleys, and standing next to her white horse, she could be the Snow Queen incognito. When her horse, nicknamed Frey, grumps at his admirers, she smiles apologetically with the grace of a diplomat and says, "He's been a tiger for a lot of years. Off and on he can be a handful." When asked if that's a desirable trait for a horse who's prancing in front of prone civilians she laughs and says, "He's an angel around people and he loves kids. Plus, he likes performing."

Kerry should know her horse. He's nearly 30 years old (Arabians are particularly long-lived) and she has owned him since he was 8. "He's been in hundreds of parades," she comments. "He knows when I finally get on him and the bands start playing that it's time. He really pumps up!"

Kerry is a veteran parader, too. She's been riding the asphalt, waving to the crowds, for almost two decades. Tonight will be her 18th appearance in the Hollywood Christmas Parade. "My mom started riding in parades in 1972," she explains. She nods in the direction of an energetic redheaded woman, who expertly combs the ringlets from Frey's cascading tail. "When I got big enough to wear her outfits, I started parading, too. I've done traditional horse showing too, but for me, parading just has a heritage, a family tradition to it."

For a moment she reminisces about the heyday of equestrian units in parades. As a child, Kerry sat in front of her TV or, if she was lucky, curbside, and was enraptured by the beautiful horses and colorful riders who danced together so confidently along the parade route. Those were the waning days of the Hollywood cowboy, when celebrities

such as Roy Rogers, Monty Montana, and Hopalong Cassidy made fancy horses, silver-encrusted saddles, and richly embroidered western clothing synonymous with parades. It seems fitting that the death of Eddie Bohlin, who designed and made so many of the classic parade saddles, and the loss of costumer and designer extraordinaire Nudie Cohn, coincided with the end of the celebrity cowboy era.

Luckily, Kerry has both a Bohlin silver saddle and a couple of rare, authentic Nudie-made outfits. "Sadly, parading is a dying hobby," she laments. "There used to be dozens of riders in various divisions," she says, referring to parades where equestrians are judged on their turnout, their attention to detail, and their personal brand of panache. When I remark that I find that difficult to believe, since I am someone who enjoys being in the spotlight with my horse, she explains, "A lot of the people who rode in parades when my mom did have retired. Their kids just didn't want to do it. It's an expensive hobby, there's no financial reward, and it takes just as much work as preparing a show horse." She clicks off her preparade routine: A week before a parade, she cleans her tack and polishes each piece of silver that decorates her hand-tooled black saddle. A couple of days later, Frey's body is shaved. The process assures that all traces of yellow are clipped away, leaving his

Opposite: Kerry Walsh's snow white horse sparkles from mane to tail.
Left: All kinds of horses participate in the parade, from ones bedecked in holiday fashions to the regal color guard.

95

"I decided I really do it for the people."

– KERRY WALSH

coat pure white. The morning before the parade, she puts together her outfit, stocks the trailer, and gives Frey a thorough shampoo. The experience is a lot of hard work on her part. So what makes her continue to parade?

"I was just thinking about it this morning," she admits. "I decided I really do it for the people. In the big cities, like here in Los Angeles, people just don't see horses. The kids especially respond to the horses. They gather around and ask questions. They always want to know if they can pet the horses, if they can just touch them. Then, on the parade route, the spectators just love to see you ride by. I can see it in their faces. They love to see how you sparkle and how beautiful the horse looks."

Paraders definitely have a calling to their passion. Jim Real, a long-time parader and a judge for equestrian units and drill teams remarks, "Paraders need to remember they're the ambassadors of the asphalt." It's a nice sentiment. For the kids who are awed at the possibility of touching a horse's velvety nose, a sequined parader mounted on a prancing steed is indeed an envoy from another world. Parade judge Kim Wehunt explains that equestrians in parades should take their mission seriously. "We want to show people that horses are more than just animals standing in a field or galloping across the prairie in a cowboy and Indian movie. They're beautiful, kind animals."

At five o'clock the riders are called to assemble at the congregation area. This represents a maelstrom of potential hazards as horses commingle with marching bands, decorated floats, and cashmere-clothed actors. Yet the horses seem to be the calmest creatures. They aren't even flustered when battery packs are tied to their saddles, powering lines of twinkle lights woven around their tack.

Leading the way is a quartet of palominos. They are not electrically embellished. They have a more somber task: they

represent the United States Marine Corps Color Guard. The large, leggy golden horses are stoic, and while their necks arch proudly, there is not a hint of unbridled spirit. With their formally attired military riders, they make a dignified impression. Adding to their mystique is the revelation that all four of the horses are former feral mustangs collected through the Bureau of Land Management's Adopt-a-Horse program. That wild horses gentled by kind human handling should be carrying the banners of their homeland makes for a warm holiday story and another memorable parade.

Opposite: Parader Kerry Walsh enjoys bringing horses to people who may have never seen them up close and personal.
Above: The horses ridden by the U.S. Marine Corps Color Guard are all former feral mustangs.

PONIES OF OUR PAST

For many young equestrians, myself included, the first pangs of passion toward horses were felt not for full-sized equines, but for their diminutive pony cousins. Because ponies are small, rotund, furry creatures with soft, liquid eyes, they are far more inviting to a child than a 1,000-pound horse. Beyond their teddy bear charm, ponies have one other child-friendly quality: they are close to the ground. It's not so scary to tumble from saddle to turf if you're only a few feet above terra firma.

Since they're descended from stock that braved harsh elements for survival, most breeds of ponies are prancing examples of the yin and yang of the equine world. Ponies are smart, yet they are also cunning. They are brave, yet they are defiant. And for every pony who is a blessing to a child's life, there is another pony who is a belligerent, crafty, evasive gremlin on four pointed hooves.

Representing one end of the pony perfection spectrum is the legacy of Pride 'n Joy, a red roan pony my girlfriend, mystery writer Laurien Berenson, owned as a child. Laurien can wax positively poetic about her pony mare. "She was the kind of pony dreams were made of," she tells me from her home in Georgia. A lifetime hunt-seat rider, Laurien has some incredible photos of her aboard the strawberry-colored pony jumping impressive obstacles at national horse shows. "She took me over fences she couldn't even see over. Her jumping style was all grace and excess energy. It never occurred to either of us that there was a jump or combination she couldn't handle."

As if Laurien's pony wasn't dreamy enough, she also possessed character. "In those days, for 10¢ you could buy a bottle of soda out of a machine. I'd open the bottle and slide the neck between her lips and her teeth on one side of her mouth. She would lift her head and tip it back and drink the whole thing."

Now that's undeniably sweet. Yet, as if to prove that there is indeed a balance within nature, I once rode the pony from the opposite end of the spectrum. I spent one summer of my youth with Michael. He was a tubby white gelding that stood about 14 hands. Someone had clipped his mane, so as it began to grow out it stood straight up like the mane of the Trojan horse. It started at his ears, which were always in some state of being pinned back, and continued thick as a broom all the way to his withers. He wasn't pretty, but he was cute in a sort of Dennis the Mennis way.

My riding instructor plucked him from a local auction because she thought he'd make a nice lesson pony for the smaller kids. Boy, was she wrong! Michael came with far more than a bad haircut. He had a repertoire of evil tricks. When I was about seventeen Michael was given to me as a project. He had frustrated my instructor because he'd become proficient at his favorite dastardly deed: About midway through a lesson, during a sprightly posting trot or a dinkity-dink pony canter, Michael would come to a halt on his own, fold up his snowy white legs like a cheap card table, and plunk to the ground. This maneuver would leave the unsuspecting child rider with a forlorn look on her face as she stood up, feet still in stirrups, over the top of the reclining pony. *The pièce de résistance*, however, came when Michael would suddenly revive himself, spring up, and dash off to the barn, leaving a dusty child in his wake.

Someone had to teach Michael that it really wasn't all that bad to live the life of a lesson pony. Because I was the resident risk-taker in the barn, always willing to climb aboard any roguish horse, the job became mine. I was tall, but I was rail thin. While my weight didn't seem to impress Michael, apparently my demeanor did. Not once did he try to lie down like a camel with me and he marched around the arena like a drone. But he was thinking of new ways to express himself all the time.

One hot August afternoon, just as I was confident I'd brainwashed him into submission, the feed truck came with its delivery. Even out in the arena I could smell the liqueur-like fragrance of cracked corn and alfalfa molasses. Michael's velvety white nose sniffled like a bunny's. With his pink lips he grabbed onto the shank of the bit, and away we went at a gallop on a beeline to the feed room. As he bolted out the arena gate, I had to swing my legs out to the side like wings to keep from being scraped off. Children scattered in fear and I yelled for help because I could see where Michael was headed. He was taking me, clinging to the saddle, to the feed room. The feed room had Dutch doors, and the top half was padlocked shut, with the bottom door open. That left just enough room for a pony to duck under and climb atop burlap bags of beckoning feed–but no clearance for his human rider.

The poor feed deliveryman, finding himself in the pathway of a runaway pony, dove for cover. I was strides from disaster when suddenly my instructor, whip in hand, appeared in the doorway. "Drat!" Michael must've thought, because he slid to a stop, whirled, and before I could extricate myself from his back, Michael bolted off to the other end of the barn. Where was I going now?

The final stall at the end of the barn housed Champ, an old buckskin gelding. He was snoozing in the corner of his home when Michael and I crashed through the canvas webbing that was snapped across the doorway. The ancient horse awoke and scrambled from his stall, wanting nothing of the chaotic proceedings. Michael, though, knew precisely what he was doing. There, in the corner of Champ's stall, was a big tub of alfalfa molasses. It drew Michael like a magnet. His head dove into the tub with such ardor that he ripped the reins out of my hands. I seized the moment and jumped from his back. I was weak-kneed and breathless, but Michael was barely warm. He paused for a brief second and raised his

head, his nose green and gooey with sweet feed, and looked at me with the hearty satisfaction only a pony can display.

My maniacal moment with Michael is legendary in local horse circles. Yet beyond the laughs he gave me, Michael taught me that some ponies have a wily spirit that's unbreakable. Michael made me examine just how much I wanted to spend my life in a saddle. Indeed, it's a testament to my love for equines that my summer with Michael didn't cool my passion. Yet in retrospect, while Laurien had her precious Pride 'n' Joy, I had my devious Michael. Who's to say which of us has the better pony tale?

Left: Many equestrians' passion is sparked by a childhood experience with a wily pony.

101

CLICK!

Being an equine photographer is fraught with professional peril. Since the horse is forever in motion, particularly at competitive events, rolls of film are consumed in an effort to snap the one shot that captures the elusive split second when horse and human coalesce into a winning team. Nearly every major horse show hosts a professional photographer. She stands guard at her chosen spot, where she has the best view of the festivities. *Click* and a blue ribbon moment, when the trophy was handed to the winner, has been documented. *Click* and a

horse's best effort in the show ring is immortalized. And yet if upon closer inspection the rider notices that her face displays a grimace, or that her horse's form is less than stellar, she will not purchase the photo. A day spent in the sun, lugging around a camera and its monstrous lens, was all for naught.

The life of equine photojournalists is tough unless the photographer is one of the few with the reputation of an artist, someone who doesn't merely hold her finger down on the automatic shutter, but who creates an image with a camera. Her pictures are indeed worth a thousand words because

Opposite: An equine photo-journalist's best work can evoke an intimate feeling. Left: Equine photo-journalists strive to capture blue ribbon moments.

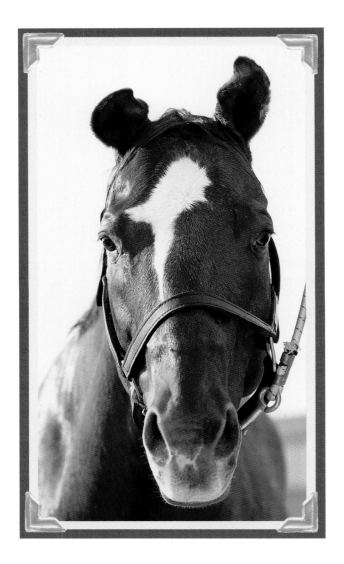

Right: A horse's personality can shine through in an ideal shot.

farm shoots, where she spends a day (or more) at a horse farm photographing the resident stallions and their off-spring for display ads, promotions, and calendar images.

In the kingdom of equine photography, Susan is a member of the royal court. Yet to speak with her, it is her love for horses, and her desire to convey their spirit and individuality, that is most evident. "I've had a passion for horses all of my life," she says in her rather quiet voice. It is slightly tinged with a Midwestern accent and she speaks deliberately, pausing before expressing herself, perhaps in the same fashion as she studies a horse before clicking the shutter.

One of her first memories of horses was when she was only four years old. Her family lived in a rural area of Illinois, and near her house was a pasture with a small herd of horses. "I never equated size with danger," Susan says, recalling how she found the horses so alluring that she once climbed into the pasture and stood still just to be near them. Soon the horses, in their typical curious manner, encircled her and dropped their heads down to sniff and nuzzle her. "I was the center of attention in this circle of horses." But soon her older sister arrived and spoiled the communion. "I remember her telling me I had to come home right then because it was dangerous to be around horses. Now, whether I said it or just thought it, I can distinctly remember the words, 'No, it isn't.' "

When Susan was nine, she got her first horse. It was a nondescript mare named Molly. "She was just this little backyard horse I rode bareback. You know, I'd put a string in her mouth and away I'd go."

Though she admits to a fascination with photos of horses, perusing treasured copies of programs from horse shows she'd attended as a child, Susan didn't begin taking photos until the early 1970s, when at the age of 37 she was given a camera as a Christmas present. At the time she was

they don't just capture a moment–they evoke a feeling. Her passion for horses comes through in glossy color.

One such photographer is Susan Sexton. Mention her name among her peers and you'll not find anyone who begrudges her the mantle of one of the elite sport horse photographers in the country. She's also sought after for living outside Scottsdale, Arizona, working for Malcolm Bricklin (the automotive entrepreneur who designed the Bricklin sports car). Among a variety of duties she cared for his string of eight horses, which he boarded at a large equestrian facility. The site, which housed over three hundred horses, was a perfect backdrop for a budding photographer. A racetrack wound its way around the stable. There was an assortment of paddocks and turnouts where horses played at liberty. And there was a steady flow of riders exercising and schooling their horses in the arenas. Susan clicked away.

"I just wandered around and took the pictures, and then showed them to people. They were more than just politely complimentary," Susan says. She had discovered her niche in the horse world, and immediately set some goals for herself. "My first goal when I started photographing horses was to become the best dressage photographer in the country. I gave myself five years. I achieved it a few years early. Of course, that's in my opinion," she laughs in a slightly self-deprecating manner. "So then I just kept polishing that skill."

Ever the evolving artist, by the late 1980s Susan began to critique her own work and found a sameness she wanted to abandon. "All my pictures looked the same, whether the horse was under saddle or turned out in a field. I felt like I was stuck in a box, and that my skills were very limited. I decided to start letting my eye and my fingers do the work and my consciousness was going to remove itself from my job."

Susan's images began to take on the impressionistic nuances she has become noted for. The horses she photographed seemed to reveal their own personalities. They were individuals now, rather than just another equine being sent through its paces. "Now what I see as a common thread in my pictures is the horses' expressions. They do that in many ways, just like humans do. They do it with the lift of an eyebrow, with a twist of an ear, with how they hold their head when they're running or walking, what they do with their tails. There are a hundred different ways a horse expresses itself, ways it expresses its temperament and character and personality."

While her passion for horses is obvious in her photos, it doesn't need to be fueled by her actually owning or riding a horse. She once lived for 12 years in an apartment above the barn at Marefield Meadows, a breeding farm for premier Hanoverians, in Warrenton, Virginia. That experience taught her that she could enjoy and appreciate the ambience of living among horses without the hands-on daily care of owning one. Yet there's no denying that horses are her life's blood.

One summer she shared her passion with her children, then aged 16, 18, and 19. The four of them piled into a house trailer and traveled the horse show circuit, clicking away for fun and profit. Susan's children got a better understanding of their mother's profession, each one becoming proficient at shooting photographs of horses. But beyond that, "It had an enormous impact on our family life, and we have maintained the fabulous relationship that was formed that summer."

When asked how the success in her career has affected her personally, Susan becomes introspective for a moment. That serendipitous event, when she was given a camera, enabled her to create a niche for herself in the world of horses. Since then, she's experienced moments she could not have dreamt of as a child awestruck with horses. One highlight she treasures was covering the equestrian competitions at the 1996 Olympic Games in Atlanta. As if befitting her stature, Susan recalls, "We, the photojournalists, were treated like royalty." She adds, "This career has made all the difference in my self-esteem. Look at it this way: People tell you how wonderful you are. And then they give you money. How much more affirmation does someone need?"

chapter
15

UP IN THE AIR

atie Lifto remembers her first attempts at riding. She struggled not with the demands of horsemanship skills, but with her diminutive size. At just five years old, it was nearly impossible for her to heave a western saddle onto one of her family's ranch horses without assistance. That perturbed the independent Katie, so she was thrilled when she was introduced to a lightweight English saddle. By the time she was six, her parents had enrolled her in English riding lessons. Katie recalls the first time she piloted the 30-year-old school horse over a tiny jump. "There was no turning back," she says. "I was thrilled with the sensation of jumping. Of course, since I'd grown up around horses I had no fear. I was this brave, gutsy little kid who'd try anything, so my riding instructors loved me."

Today, Katie Lifto is a professional horse trainer and English riding instructor based in southern California. Her ultimate goal is to be a star on the Grand Prix circuit, where corporate sponsorships buoy up cash prizes in the tens of thousands of dollars and the jumps reach the size of small houses. "There really isn't anything I don't like about competing," she says. Not even the grind of moving from one motel to the other or the lack of home cooked meals? Not the roller coaster of maintaining competitive zeal when you win a blue ribbon and a check one day, but face disappointment the next? "Nope," she says emphatically, adding a smile of reassurance. "Last year we spent months on the road, hauling my Grand Prix horse from show to show, driving cross-country. It was just me, Joe [her husband and coach], the horse, and the dog. It was great!"

The payoff for competitors such as Katie has to be more than blue ribbons and a split of the prize money. A simple explanation might be that horse shows attract people with a competitive streak in their personalities. After

all, riders perform in an arena against their peers and are ranked accordingly. Some people just have that compulsion to prove to themselves that they're number one. But for jumper riders there's a bigger lure: the chance to be up in the air, suspended above earth for a moment as horse and human leap together. To the nonrider, the feat of a

*Opposite: Katie Lifto
competes when she is
not training.
Left: Trainer Katie Lifto
never looked back once
she experienced
the excitement of
show jumping.*

"She and I have a bond that I've never experienced with another horse."

– MOIRA HARRIS

huge animal soaring over a dozen human-made obstacles appears dangerous. But by the time horse and rider enter the show arena, years of preparation have made them ready for the challenges of flight. There's no finer sensation than meeting a jump at the perfect point of takeoff and flying through the air on the back of a trusty mount.

Amateur adult jumper rider Moira Harris still recalls the first time she jumped a horse. "The first jump I ever experienced was from the back of my favorite old lesson horse, a Thoroughbred named High Fleet. He was a direct descendant of Triple Crown winner Count Fleet, but High Fleet was a raw-boned, parrot-mouthed gelding," she recalls fondly. "I must've been about 10 years old. I'd been practicing my jumping position in lessons for a couple of days and it was time to put it to the test. The fence was probably just a cross rail, not anything the horse couldn't have just trotted over. But High Fleet gave a little hop over the jump and I clung to his back like a monkey, hands planted firmly on the jump strap buckled around his neck. It was exciting!"

Though she spent years riding hunters, where the fences and courses are as inviting as an afternoon canter across the countryside, Moira never considered venturing into the realm of show jumping. "I remember watching jumper rounds at horse shows, seeing the height and the wild color of the fences, the boldness of the horses and riders, the aggressiveness it took to win and thinking, 'Boy, that will never be me.' And yet here I am, in my late 30s, riding in show jumping classes." She pauses, rolls her eyes, and laughs. "I must be crazy!"

Actually, it was Moira's Irish Thoroughbred mare who chose the jumper career path. Typical of her heritage, the tall, lanky bay mare had a brave, hardy nature and a dedicated work ethic. The mundane earth tone fences in the hunter arena bored her; she relished the challenges of the jumper courses.

"She's a jumper through and through," Moira confides, wholly supportive of the notion that a true horseman finds a job that best suits the talents of the horse. "When she's on course, her ears are always forward, looking for that next fence."

Unfortunately, things don't always go as planned in the world of show jumping. These are events judged objectively, where numerical faults are calculated for rails that are knocked down, hooves that take a dip in the water jump, and rounds that exceed the prescribed time limit. To win at show jumping, horses and riders must be clean over the course and they must do it without hesitation because the clock is ticking. A dismal performance can be humbling, especially when it includes cascading jump poles and a rider being dumped onto wet turf. "When I make a mistake," Moira reveals, "it's usually a boneheaded one. What's bad for me is to dwell on it, to focus on something I did that was a stupid mistake. I need to immediately move on and get to the next round." Fortunately, her mare has a forgiving nature. "She and I have a bond that I've never experienced with another horse. She's saved my skin on more than one occasion."

Katie agrees that when you're competing on the show jumping circuit, you must possess a thick skin and the determination of a committed athlete to persevere through the rough times. "You can be on top of the world one moment, and the next round things just go wrong on course."

How do Katie, Moira, and others who are dedicated high fliers maintain their desire to compete yet again? "The world of show jumping can be very humbling at times. You have to be passionate about the sport, passionate about horses to stick with it." Katie thinks for a moment and then adds, "I love my life. I have to do this. I'm with the horses every day. Even on my days off I come to the barn. Horses are more than my job, more than my hobby. They're my whole identity."

Opposite: Amateur show jumper Moira Harris says her horse is a natural-born jumper.

THE WONDER HORSE

On most Saturday afternoons, my cousins and I would sit cross-legged on warm cement and watch Jack Dutton and his trick horse, Serrano, perform at a local western-themed amusement park. I was enraptured by the way Jack could communicate with the big brown horse. Old Serrano seemed to know the answer to simple questions, nodding yes or shaking his mane no. And he could do math. Jack would put forth a short equation and Serrano would flick his ears, thinking for a moment, then lower his head and pick up a numbered block with his big yellow teeth. Of course the wooden block was embellished with the right answer. How did Jack communicate with Serrano? What was that secret language they shared? I envisioned that if I ever owned such a wondrous animal, I too could master the private code that allowed select humans to speak to horses.

Years later I learned that Serrano, like trick horses before and after him, was trained to respond to subtle cues of body language and facial expressions given by his handler. Still, that didn't dampen my appreciation for this peculiar equestrian art, even if it relied on a little bit of chicanery. I've

Opposite: Tonka performs a signature move. Left: Tex Choate and horse Tonka seem to communicate on a higher level.

owned horses for 30 years and I still cannot compel them to move their thousand pounds of body mass off my toes when they decide to stand atop my feet.

In my travels, I came across another man who also speaks that secret language to horses. His name is Tex Choate, and his current trick horse is a flashy, sleek-coated overo pinto with the stage name of Tonka the Wonder Horse. That's quite a mouthful, but fortunately the star is comfortable with the general public referring to him as plain old Tonka.

On a decidedly hot summer day, Tex casually slips a braided red halter onto the gelding's head and leads him out into the sunshine. Without much ado, the tall laconic man in the cowboy hat puts Tonka through several acts: bowing, kneeling, lying down, saying yes or no, and giving Tex a big, slobbery kiss. There is no chain attached to the lead rope to grate against the horse's muzzle, no sharp object that pokes or prods the pinto into submission. Tonka observes his handler with keen eyes, focusing on subtle cues from the motion of a hand or the feather-light tickle of a short whip. "I never hit a horse," Tex offers. "There's no reason to." When asked how he got such willing responses from Tonka he replies, "Are you married?"

I nod yes.

"Well, haven't you learned how to cleverly motivate your husband?"

I figure at that point the secret language I was seeking was perhaps a universal one and not so exclusive after all. "I see. So it's basically the art of gentle persuasion."

Tex explains that first of all, a prospective trick horse needs to be sensitive so he will respond to the faintest cue, one no stronger than the minute annoyance of a fly landing on his skin. Then he must be intelligent so he has the ability to focus on new tasks and retain them. Training sessions are kept short, because the typical horse has a very short attention span. Additionally, the horse must have a nature kind enough to allow him to bond with his human handler. Finally, immediate reward, usually in the form of a loving pat, reinforces the lesson. "Horses are just like people," Tex says. "They like to have approval if they do something right."

Tonka is winning lots of approval lately, currently makes the rounds of birthday parties and other celebrations, offering his services to crowds of giddy children, most of them impassioned with a severe case of equine mania. But Tex also devotes much of Tonka's time to charitable work. Recently he and Tonka were part of the annual Jerry Lewis MDA Telethon, providing entertainment for the children. When complimented on his devotion, Tex looks a bit puzzled at the accolade and then says softly, "Well, you have to give something back, especially to those sorts of kids."

It's clear that Tex savors his life with horses, whether he is giving back to the community or simply enjoying a ride. He was born 70 years ago in Oklahoma. His father was a farmer so Tex is well acquainted with workhorses. His first job with horses came at the tender age of 5 when he boldly inquired about earning some money with the foreman of a local construction job. The fellow had a team of draft horses who were pulling felled logs off the land. Tex got a job sitting atop the broad backs of the horses, holding the reins and steering the team.

As a young teen he worked as an auctioneer tending cattle. He later moved on to the rodeo circuit, where he became fascinated with the antics of the clowns, who deftly cajoled the bulls and entertained the crowds by doing stunts with some of the horses. "I'd go up and just ask the clowns, 'How did you do that?' And then I'd put it all together myself."

Opposite: Tonka responds to gentle cues from Tex to perform tricks like bowing.

"There will never be another Chick."

— TEX CHOATE

His first endeavor was with a hybrid equine, a mule to be specific. "You know mules are stubborn, but this one was out of a hackney mare so he was very sensitive. When I'd touch him, he'd move. This was a real one-man mule," Tex says with an audible chuckle, recounting how his mule act got integrated into the rodeo's performance. "They'd put the mule in a corral and the announcer would say, 'Well, now, you young cowboys come out and put a saddle on him,' like a contest. But of course they couldn't even catch him! So then the announcer would see me and say, 'Here's another volunteer, folks. Let's see this old man give it a try.' I'd come out and just slap my leg, and the mule would walk right up to me and give me a big kiss. And then I'd put a saddle on him and ride him around the whole arena without a bridle on him." Tex's ruse with the mule always brought the crowd to its feet.

In the 1980s, Tex was working a job clearing land in a southern California suburb and became enamored with a sorrel Morgan filly stabled on the property. He bought the flashy yearling, thinking right away that she had all the makings of a future trick horse. Because she balked slightly while loading in the trailer, one of the handlers scolded the filly with the admonition, "You'd better not kick me, chick." Tex liked the sound of that and christened the red horse with the flaxen mane Chick.

Over the years, Tex and Chick were inseparable. He hauled her around wherever he went, often taking her along on jobs clearing trees. "I just wanted her to be with me," he says. The mare enjoyed the sojourns. "Pretty soon she thought she was part of me."

Sure enough, Chick became an exemplary trick horse. She even earned roles in movies and an appearance on a popular television sitcom of that era, *Full House*. The mare's résumé made her even more popular with the birthday party crowds, where she often performed her trademark stunt. "I could shoot a cap gun and she'd fall down and play dead," Tex says. "Then I'd have the kids gather around and we'd say a little prayer and then suddenly Chick would spring back to life."

The Morgan mare enjoyed the spotlight, but she was no prissy starlet. She was also a working cow horse, and in 1989 Tex won the U.S. Team Penning Association National Finals aboard her. Other competitors, aware of Chick's talents, teased Tex that the mare could read the numbers pasted on the hides of the cattle so she knew which ones she was supposed to cut from the herd. Tex admits he played into the teasing. He tells how he'd leave Chick loose, about a quarter of a mile away from his trailer, then he would nonchalantly whistle and the mare would gallop up to him. It was that level of trust and communication that made theirs a rare partnership.

One day Tex came home from work and found Chick taking her final breaths. "The vet stayed up with her all night, but he couldn't save her. I think, to this day, that someone poisoned her." It's unusual for a young, healthy horse to suddenly becoming so violently ill. He contemplates his role in the demise of his beloved mare. Maybe he made her too famous. Maybe someone was jealous. Regardless of the culprit, Chick was gone. There was no magic word to resurrect her this time. Not bearing to part with her, Tex buried the mare on his ranch.

Though he has the spotted wonder horse, Tonka, and a chunky quarter horse named Bear who perform a routine of amazing tricks, neither will replace Chick. When asked if the sudden loss of the mare broke his heart, Tex's blue eyes mist over with a discernible cloud of gray and he sighs, "There will never be another Chick."

Opposite: The sudden death of Chick, Tex's mare, broke his heart.

17

A Member
of the Family

If a horse is well cared for, blessed with vigor and sound conformation, he can live a comfortable, useful life well into his 20s. Of course, he may be afflicted with the same maladies that affect humans of advancing age, namely digestive upsets and arthritis. Yet while humans might shuttle off dowager aunts to the local retirement village, many horse lovers are reluctant to say good-bye to an aging equine. When fortunate enough to afford continuing care, they'll go to great lengths to accommodate just about any level of decrepitude. In our urbanized and asphalt-paved society, that adage about a retired horse being turned out to pasture is becoming a dream. There is simply very little lush pastureland sitting idle, available for such use. Fortunate enough to reside in towns zoned for horsekeeping, Mistry and Ziggy are two of the lucky beasties who are ensconced in the role of four-legged lawn ornament.

Mistry's owner is Paul Chapman, an affable guy whose job as an audio technician in the television industry often elicits prodding inquiries. "Yeah, everyone always wants to know where the mikes get hidden on certain stars. How we tape them in place. It's a tough job," he quips, "but someone's got to do it."

He brings the same laid-back sense of humor to his 22-year relationship with his sorrel mare, Mistry. "If you had told me two decades ago that I'd still own this horse, I'd have said you were crazy. I guess I somehow figured her life span would be something similar to a dog's. But," he says, stroking the horse's deep red coat with a brush, "here we still are." With a frosting of white hair around her muzzle and eyes, the 25-year-old mare stands languidly while Paul grooms her. He won't ride her today. Despite a set of orthopedic horseshoes, which need to be replaced every six to eight weeks at a cost of over $100, her arthritis is flaring up. So he'll just snap a lead rope on her and stroll along the trails with her, walking alongside like a supportive companion. "When she was younger, I'd

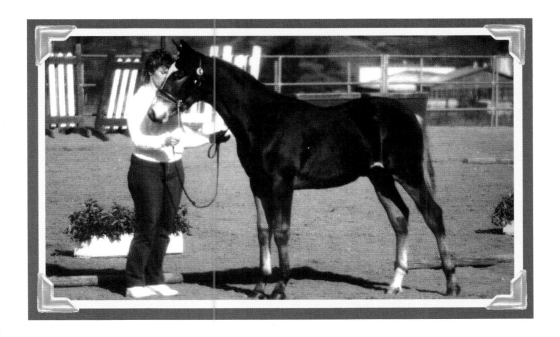

take her out for five-hour trail rides. We'd be gone all day. It was great. But now, if she's feeling good, we'll maybe go out for an hour two or three times a week. And no galloping. We just walk and trot a little. She thinks she wants to run. But she'll take a few steps at the gallop and I can feel her think, *Ah, maybe that wasn't a good idea.*"

Though he had ridden horses off and on while growing up in a Los Angeles suburb, Paul didn't dream of owning his own horse until he rode with a friend from work. "He had a couple of horses boarded north of LA and asked me to come for a ride." The place was also home to a rental string, where urban dwellers could pay a few dollars and ride a horse along a well-worn trail for an hour. Paul was intrigued by a young red mare the proprietor's young son was riding. "This kid was using a three-year-old mare to push the rent string out on the trail," he explains, saying that without such urging the throng of wily, barn sour horses would whirl around at the river bed

Opposite: Though Paul Chapman's day job is as an audio technician, his passion is his horse, Mistry. Above: Ziggy enjoys the good life in spite of blindness.

125

"The second month I owned her I had to nurse her through a major bout of colic. I wanted to put some weight on her, so I took some free advice and began free-feeding her alfalfa molasses." Though giving a thin horse constant access to sweet feed is a method for packing on calories, Mistry grew up fending for herself among a herd of aggressive older horses. Suddenly, having an endless supply of food was more than she could handle and she gorged herself. "That was my big lesson about not taking tips from just one source, especially not an authoritative one."

Next came an initiation to horsemanship skills. "I admit it, my riding skills were pretty much kick, go, and stop," he says, almost shaking his head in embarrassment. "The turning point was when my girlfriend, who is far more educated about horses, started telling me better ways to do things. I started working Mistry in a round pen, teaching her to respond to voice commands." His biggest accomplishment? "The day she understood 'whoa' meant stop."

As the years progressed, Paul began to develop a personal bond with the mare. One December, during a horrible rainy season, Mistry's paddock at the boarding stable became partially flooded. Not wanting his cherished mare to slog through mud to reach the water trough at the back of the corral, Paul made a ritual of bringing her five gallons of water, bucket by bucket, each morning at six and each evening at six. "She'd wait for me and meet me at the gate to her corral and drink the water I brought her. Then I'd walk away feeling better, knowing that she was warm and dry. I did this for an entire month. Then one night I was an hour late. I was in a panic. I got there at seven o'clock and you know what I found? One set of fresh tracks going out through the mud to the water trough, and one set of tracks coming back. And a horse with mud up to her knees."

And what did that teach him, beyond the fact that Mistry knew quite well how to ease her thirst? "Well, I'm not an

and gallop back to the stable with their powerless tinhorn riders. Something about the mare's spirit and obvious kind nature struck Paul's fancy. He asked to ride her regularly. "The owner of the place wasn't really fond of her," Paul recalls. "They liked to rope and work cattle, and Mistry didn't seem interested in that. Plus, she was underweight and scrawny. She just wasn't cut out for working cows. So one day the owner told me I might as well buy her since I was riding her all the time anyway."

Most of Paul's horse care skills with his new horse came via trial and error. Thankfully, Mistry has an iron constitution.

idiot. I realize she's an animal and that maybe to her I'm just the guy who brings the water. Or the guy with the food. But that's okay, because I get so much out of the relationship. I don't have any kids, and Mistry gives me an opportunity to take care of something that can't take care of itself, and I think there's value in that. So yeah, I'm a guy who enjoys nurturing. Besides," he says, patting the mare on her ample, crested neck, "by now she's like a member of the family."

Another horse enjoying family status among passionate horse lovers is a bay gelding named Ziggy. He is 17 years old. And for two years he has been blind.

"My neighbor swears that Ziggy can still see something, because he'll pluck an orange off his tree and hold it over the fence and Ziggy will trot up and eat it out of his hand," relates Debbie Bisbee. She pauses between feeding Ziggy handfuls of snacks and recounts how she came to own a sightless horse.

"I was born in Iowa," she says in a voice still touched with the sweetness of a Midwestern accent, "and my father worked on a farm. He takes credit for putting me up on my very first horse when I was just a real little girl. I was so horse-crazy. But my parents couldn't afford one. When I got married and moved to California, I vowed to have a horse before I turned 30."

She began by taking English riding lessons and learning to jump. She did that on the back of an Appaloosa gelding. "I liked him so much that I told my instructor to go find me a horse just like him. And you know what? She did! It was a big, stout appy mare named Josie."

Debbie and Josie were champions in the amateur hunter division, an accomplishment since colorful horses were often frowned upon in the traditional realm of bays and chestnuts. "When it was time to retire Josie, I decided to breed her. I chose a Trakehner warmblood stallion. He seemed like the perfect match."

"I've always understood him and accepted his flaws. Maybe he's my version of the ultimate problem child."

– DEBBIE BISBEE

The resultant foal was Ziggy, and right from the start he was full of mischief. "He jumped up when he was just a few minutes old and started running around the stall. We were trying to snap pictures and he'd dart in and out between Josie's legs and kick at us. He was like a hyperactive child. We knew we had ourselves a live wire."

To teach him discipline, Debbie began working with Ziggy as soon as he was broke to lead in a halter. She taught him to trot beside her and stand at attention. By the time he was ready to start under saddle, he'd been to a number of shows, winning blue ribbons in halter competition. Though he worked well with Debbie, not everyone could ride Ziggy. And not everyone wanted to. More than one professional trainer refused to work with him because true to his earlier indications, he could be rambunctious under tack. Yet when given an interesting job, Ziggy was a solid performer. He became a member of an all-Trakehner drill team that performed dressage and jumping routines set to music. Off stage his antics earned him less than rave reviews. "He was notorious for ducking out of his stall or yanking his head free of his halter and then just taking off for a spin around the show grounds."

When he wasn't on the road, Ziggy lived in a comfortable stable in Debbie's backyard. One evening, she just happened to notice that his eyes looked strange. "There was this whitish rectangle where his pupils should've been," she recalls. "At first I wanted to deny it, but then I had to admit I was having trouble at the canter with him. He'd walk and trot fine, but he'd take a few strides at the canter and suddenly halt. That was so unlike him. So I had the vet out and he diagnosed advanced cataracts in both of Ziggy's eyes. I can still hear the vet saying, 'He'll continue to lose sight and go blind.' It was something I'll never forget."

Debbie and her husband, George, consulted with a leading veterinary ophthalmologist who had performed a number of successful cataract surgeries on large animals, including horses. Though Ziggy was considered an aged horse, he qualified as a good surgical candidate, so Debbie and George decided to put up the $3,000 for the operation on one eye.

For the first two weeks after the lengthy operation, Ziggy proved he'd regained some sight. But things soon went downhill, despite optimum care. "Let's just say that every complication that could happen, happened, including an allergic reaction to the sutures in his eye."

Because Ziggy was raised in Debbie's backyard, the bay knows his way around his environment, perhaps much like a sightless human learns to count steps from one landmark to another. His biggest adjustment has been learning to rely more on other horses and on Debbie herself. That's not easy for a horse who tends to scoff at humans in the role of authority figure.

"Another big adjustment was that Ziggy always saw himself as the leader of the herd, but now he depends on his girlfriends to keep him secure." She motions toward two Thoroughbred mares who serve as companions. "The first winter he was terrified because of the sound of rain hitting the metal roof of his stall. I guess he'd never paid attention to it. But now with his girlfriends, he's fine. He seems to sense their presence even if they're not nose-to-nose. And then he's learned to rely on me. He used to be rather aloof, but now he listens to my voice. If he starts to get upset, I can calm him down by speaking to him."

For a horse who earned a reputation for being full of shenanigans, Ziggy is enjoying retirement in the backyard of a loving owner. "I guess I feel he's my responsibility," Debbie says. "If it weren't for me breeding his mother, he wouldn't have been born." She reaches over and pats the horse's blazed face. "I've always understood him and accepted his flaws. Maybe he's my version of the ultimate problem child."

Opposite: Debbie Bisbee's horse, Ziggy, gets around in spite of his blindness.

ALL THE PRETTY (MODEL) HORSES

Remember that scene in *The Wizard of Oz* where Dorothy first steps from her tornado-transported house into the land of the munchkins? The environment was strikingly surreal, and though the scenery was familiar–flowers, foliage, and that inescapable yellow brick road–it was unearthly. Dorothy was astounded. She most certainly wasn't in Kansas anymore. Such is the feeling when Sharon, the photographer of this book, and I step inside the exposition hall at the Los Angeles County Fairgrounds that housed the 11th Annual West Coast Model Horse Collector's Jamboree. We are expecting haphazard displays of those plastic model horses that nearly every youthful horse lover gets as the traditional holiday gift. Yet what we see before us eclipses any childhood exercises with make-believe plastic ponies. These folks are serious about their hobby. And we are the strangers in a strange land.

Tables stretch from one end of the warehouse-sized building to the other, and each supports rows of pristine models, many of them posing in mid-prance. The first table supports groupings of private collections that resem-

TRICKED OUT PONY

Opposite: Model horse shows can be just as serious as those that feature live animals. Left: A participant in the "Tricked Out" category.

133

ble herds segregated not by fence lines but by the out-stretched arms of the humans who guard them. Those horses not allowed to roam freely are sequestered inside homemade stables constructed of cardboard or, if they reside at a tabletop hunt club, of wood veneer. Some horses stand transfixed, perhaps eyeing the invisible stable boy coming toward them with the day's ration of grain. The more spirited ones, those whose heads are turned slightly back, one leg curled and raised above the ground, tail aloft, are tethered lest they bolt and run. Sharon and I are trans-fixed. "And yet, not a pawer or a cribber among them," I note dryly. "Might I remind you," Sharon says nudging me, "they aren't real."

We walk to an alcove set apart from the midway where a blond woman sits with the aplomb of a Texan baroness admiring her bloodstock. With little prodding she begins to explain how the value of a collectible horse figu-rine is determined. There is the rarity of the model, its preserved condition, and whether or not it has been enhanced or retouched. When I ask for more explanation on that, she points out examples of mundane creations (think ordinary nags) that have been transformed into flashier forms with the skillful application of some paint. A few strokes of white acrylic and a plain bay sports white stockings and a blaze.

But wait—there's more. She lifts a sheet of bubble wrap and unveils an exquisite figurine. This is no plastic horse. It is a resin model, she explains, that begins life as a clay sculpture, is cast in a resin mold, and then is hand-painted by a renowned model artist. The horse is a pinto, mostly alabaster white but with large patches of taupe brown mottled with dapples. She encourages me to peek at the belly of this fawnlike statue, which, I can see, is a delicate rendering of a yearling saddlebred. There is the artist's name, signed as if the figurine were a Rembrandt. It is just as lovely. In the same manner I would use to reach forward to stroke the mane of a live horse who caught my fancy, I put thumb and forefinger to resin and lift the figurine from its mattress of bubble wrap.

The blond woman bolts upright in her chair, one hand to her chest and the other to her gaping mouth. She looks to be suffering a fit of apoplexy. "Oh! Oh! Please set it down! Please don't handle it! That's a $700 dollar horse!"

Having once held the reins of Brentina, a flesh and blood Olympic dressage horse worth $1 million, I am a little taken aback by the woman's reaction. But I comply, laying the little saddlebred back on its bed and raising my hands, palms open, like a bank robber relinquishing the loot. Sharon leans over and whispers in my ear. "Step away from the pretty horsey."

There is an audible crackle over the PA system and I am certain I can decipher the words "horse show." The competition is starting. We find our way to yet another long table, where two rows of plastic horses prance in formation. In some fashion, it much resembles a true-life show: The judge, looking contemplative, holds a clipboard in her hands and is making furtive notes about each entry. One frazzled teen, with an angst-skewed face, begs to be permitted to add her horse to the lineup because she was back at the concession stand and didn't hear the final call. The judge thinks for a moment and relents.

The judge's name is Christie Partee. She is from Grapevine, Texas. She smiles and introduces herself as the president of the North American Model Horse Shows Association. I ask her to explain just what she is judging and how the ribbons will be awarded.

The class is for horses manufactured only by Stone Company, a model horse manufacturer. The type of horse is limited to solid-colored stock horses or quarter horses. There are 65 entries frozen in parade stance before her. Christie's task seems as difficult as that of a judge officiating over a western pleasure class at the American Quarter Horse Association World Championship Show.

"First thing I look for is condition, to see if the horse has any missing paint, scratches, or blemishes. That's going to knock it out of competition at this level. The next thing I look at is rarity. That sort of information, those facts, I have to know in my head," she says, explaining that some models had a limited run. She points to one horse and says, "That was a special run that was put out four years ago." When I remark that I sometimes have trouble remembering the age and pedigrees of my oat-burning horses, she winks and says, "It's a learned art."

I ask her which color is most desirable in a plastic model horse. She replies, "Well, there's personal preference. Do I like buckskin? Do I like dun?" Both colors are variations on a theme: a tan horse with a darker mane and tail. Yet apparently, such nuances can matter. This is turning out to be more of a parallel universe than I had anticipated. "Huh. So you mean the judging is partly subjective, just like a real-life horse show?" I ask, trying to keep hidden the sting from last weekend's horse show, when the judge continually pinned a black horse over my bay mare. "Yes, there are a lot of similarities," she says.

As I inspect the rows of horses, acting unofficially as backseat judge, I see no flaws, no scuffmarks, and no missing paint. "How are these show horses maintained? They look so new. My real show horses should look so good." Christie lowers her clipboard and speaks quietly, as if revealing secret information. "Personally, my show horses stay packed. I live in Texas, and I'm a little fearful of natural disasters."

Opposite: Some model horses can go for hundreds of dollars.

"*I like the two worlds to intersect.*"

– Sheryl Leisure

"You mean tornadoes and floods?"

"Those, yes. And cat attacks."

"Pardon?"

"Model horse people usually have cats, and cats are known to enjoy climbing shelves…" Christie doesn't finish her sentence, but she wrinkles her face and gives the same look someone might express when viewing a train wreck.

After taking Christie away from her official duties, Sharon and I leave the judging arena and head for the vendor's row. Several artists display their handmade western tack, perfectly sized to fit the standard model horse. The intricacies can be astounding. Each western saddle is built upon its own preformed tree. Working western saddles, those for the stock horses, are identical to those a cowboy uses to ride the range, right down to hand-tooled leather, hand-braided lariat, rope cinch, and woolen Navajo saddle blanket. Tiny bits, silver concho buttons, and buckles are poured from exclusive molds and made of pewter. For the more extravagant saddlebred models, one-of-a-kind parade saddles and bridles are available. Pewter trimmings, looking like authentic silver trappings, are etched in a scroll design. I inquire about the cost for such made-to-order tack. The parade saddle perched on the palomino before me is about $450. I don't touch it.

Sharon and I are beginning to realize that a whole other world of horse lovers exists. Most of these people don't own a real horse, but that doesn't cool their passion. They have merely found another way of expressing it. So what if their hands might not soothe the damp neck of a spirited horse? They love all things equine no less. And sometimes, their love is expressed in a wildly artistic manner.

In the center of the exposition hall is a display called Tricked Out Ponies. After studying the entries in this contest, we both decide it rivals the floral designers' contests at county fairs, where competitors go just a tad overboard with their arrangements of flowers, stems, Styrofoam, and vases. The challenge here is to create a unique statement in art, using a traditional Breyer horse model. There is a Trojan horse, complete with ladder, trapdoor, and tiny Greeks hanging from ropes. Another horse has undergone meticulous reconstructive surgery to be transformed into a Tiffany-inspired nightlight. But our favorite is the jewel-toned entry called The Gift Horse. An erstwhile saddlebred model has been transformed into a sort of candy dish. The wavy plastic mane and tail are gone, replaced by curved copper wire bejeweled with glass beads. It is an explosion of color and inspiration tempered with humor.

To end our day, I chat with Sheryl Leisure, who organized the event. Since I am still a bit overwhelmed, I ask her to describe the typical collector and jamboree participant. "I'd say the average model hobbyist is a woman 30 to 50 years old. She has a 50 percent chance of owning a real horse. Generally, she has a loving husband or significant other who sits back and lets her do this 'thing,' and then with events like this they come along to see just what it is she does."

Sheryl's mission is to use her savvy and talent to merge the world of the model horse people with that of the real horse world. "I'd like the two worlds to intersect," she says. To reach that goal, she's creating and marketing her own line of horse figurines and sculptures, even allowing equestrians to have resin sculptures painted to match the markings of their own living, breathing horses. A die-hard collector, she herself has over three thousand models. She shows me a photo of the entire herd, poised for action upon a roomful of shelves. I think of the potential for natural disaster with that many models and wonder out loud if she owns any cats.

She reaches down and brushes white hair from her black blouse. "I have four."

Opposite: Event organizer Sheryl Leisure says that for many, collecting models fill the need for people who never had live horses.

A WINNING
COMBINATION

"There's always that opportunity of the next race."

— CLARE BAZLEY

It's only 7:00 A.M. but already the Los Alamitos Race Course, in California, is alive with activity. At one end of the straightaway—called the chute—there is a small starting gate of four stalls. Here, young horses are being schooled to approach the cagelike contraption. It undoubtedly looks menacing to a horse fresh in from the farm. But these are quarter horses, bred to run sprint races. They must break from the gate at full speed and blast their way to the finish line a few hundred yards dead ahead. A balk when the gates open or a stumble at the start surely means the horse has lost all chance for a paycheck.

At mid-track, a collection of trainers and assistants sit upon their placid saddle horses, many of them retired racehorses themselves who were kind enough (or in some instances cantankerous enough) to find a second career accompanying fractious racehorses to their morning workouts. Though they're referred to as lead ponies, they are full-sized brawny horses. These equine babysitters pay little attention to their charges other than to occasionally nip or pin their ears in rebuke if one of the athletes gets too rambunctious. Otherwise, they barely flick an ear even when some of the quarter horses, primed for a race and aching to run, are set off at an awe-inspiring gallop by their exercise riders.

At a nod from the trainer, the exercise rider merely rises from the saddle, assuming the classic jockey-styled perch, and the horse stiffens his tail, reaches forward like a stag with his front legs, and digs into the sandy loam of the track with both hind hooves. In a few ferocious bounds, he has achieved full speed. The incredible display of instant power is made possible by the horse's brawny hindquarters. These horses obviously relish the opportunity to express their true nature: to run.

Clare Bazley rides onto the track next. She's aboard her red roan lead pony with the quirky name of Rambling Barstool. "We just call him Barstool," she says with a smile, as if that's as suitable a handle as Red or Rambler or Barney. This morning, she is ponying a devilishly handsome young stallion with a coat the color of cola. His name is Chocolate Rocket, and the name fits. In fact, the exercise rider aboard the stallion has a hard time keeping the brown horse under control. "He's fully conditioned and ready to race. We want to keep him fresh," Clare explains. So she instructs the exer-

Opposite: Clare Bazley helps condition horses for racing. Above: The Bazleys make racing a way of life.

"Beginning in February, the two-year-olds come in from the farms. They need conditioning before they can race. They need to get schooled in the starting gate, and they need to get used to the grandstand," he explains. Even though many of the youngsters have had a basic education at a farm, they must get used to the dizzying activity at the track. "The actual surface of the track is new to them, too," Tom says.

Because quarter horse racing offers most of its biggest purses to two-year-olds, there can be pressure from some owners to get their prospects qualified for the big races, even when Tom knows better. The same holds true for older horses who are falling off their racing form and are perhaps past their prime. "If I don't want to run a horse anymore or think it's best for the horse to retire, if the owners want to keep running him they need to go some-place else. Fortunately, I don't have those sorts of clients. I don't end up keeping ones like that."

In fact, rather than burning out a precocious young horse, Tom is adamant that he'd rather bring the horse along slowly so that he can remain sound and productive when mature. "To me, there's nothing more rewarding than having a good older horse in the barn." And what's the future for those horses who are retired? "Some are sold as jumpers. Others make really nice saddle horses. And then many go on to do barrel racing or gymkhana," he says, explaining that a small, speedy quarter horse is perfect for many types of competitive rodeo events.

As Tom discusses the wide variety of options for his charges, it's apparent that he enjoys his profession. He has held his professional trainer's license since 1982. A native of Connecticut, he was introduced to the world of horse racing by his brother, who encouraged him to come out to California to give life at the racetrack a try. Not only did Tom find early success, inheriting a few solid runners

Above: The Bazleys say they would not trade the ups and downs of training for a nine-to-five job.

cise rider to merely let the colt stretch his legs first by strolling up one length of the track, then trotting a few paces, and then finish by leisurely cantering down the back-stretch. This is Clare's job at the training stable she runs with her husband Tom. Later that morning, she'll pony a young chestnut filly who is recovering from a sore heel.

Back at the barn, while the horses nibble mid-morning snacks of Timothy hay from hay nets suspended just outside their stalls, Tom Bazley chats with the track vet. The horses running tonight get a cursory inspection to make sure they're fit to compete. Then Tom walks into the tack room and puts tags on the bridles for the three horses who will race under the bright stadium lights. Doing so ensures that a groom won't hastily grab the wrong equipment for a horse. Right now the atmosphere around the barn is relaxed and there is time to chat about the more hectic spring season—when he'll be hit with an onslaught of two-year-olds.

from the man with whom he'd apprenticed, but he also found his wife, Clare.

The brunette with the effervescent eyes rides up to the barn as if on cue. A horse lover all her life, Clare began working as a groom for a racehorse trainer right after high school. She continued working at the track during the summers while she attended college. The quarter horse racing circuit was incorporated into the various county fairs up and down the coast of California. Like a racetrack gypsy, Clare followed. "I lived in the barns, in the tack room. The fairs moved every two weeks. I had a little hatchback car, and I could pack up my tack room accessories in the back of my car. You know, the basic essentials: a folding bed and a little toaster oven."

To earn extra money, Claire also worked a stint as a groom for the irrepressible, notable trainer D. Wayne Lukas at Thoroughbred racetracks such as Santa Anita. "I had three horses I was in charge of. That's the limit in his barn; the ratio of horses to grooms. I started at five o'clock every morning." When she decided to take a job closer to home, near the San Francisco Bay area, she journeyed up to the track at Bay Meadows, where the quarter horses were running. She gained a job as a barn foreman. As luck would have it, her new place of employment was directly across the barn aisle from Tom Bazley's training stable. Using racetrack lingo, Clare laughingly admits that she put her eyes on Tom and decided she had to claim him.

Though horses are her passion, Clare decided she needed another outlet to express herself. "I've always been involved in art; painting, drawing, making crafty things. I also have this little entrepreneurial impulse within me." She began making colorful, vintage-styled Bakelite jewelry for herself, but she soon had a following of admirers. An intriguing side effect was that her customers also wanted "anything and everything buttons," she says. So about 10 years ago, she began amassing an impressive collection of rare artistic buttons, many of them collectible antiques, transforming a portion of them into jewelry. Again, her customer base increased. She soon became known as the "button lady," a moniker she's determined to bestow upon a quarter horse filly. Needless to say, a vast portion of her unique button and handmade jewelry collection features equestrian imagery. There are scrimshaw etchings of galloping horses, cameos of mares and foals, traditional English hunt scene prints, glazed metallic horse heads, and small bronzed medallions featuring horses and riders. Who knew so many horse-inspired buttons existed?

Tom is quick to interject that there are times when being a racehorse trainer begins to look less appealing than, say, marketing handcrafted jewelry. "When it gets frustrating, I think about how I could be working a nine-to-five job and probably make the same amount of money," he says, revealing that "unless you have good horses in the barn, you aren't going to make that much money." Then he pauses, looks about him, and says, "But then, why would I want to walk away from this?"

The final parade of horses is returning from the morning workouts. Invigorated by the exercise, the horses make a metallic staccato rhythm on the coarse asphalt as they prance. Their riders reach down to soothe them with a pat upon their arched necks. It's easy to understand how such a panorama of color, sound, and barely bridled athleticism becomes addictive.

Clare expresses the optimism that keeps both Tom and her in the racehorse business. Even if one of their horses fails to earn a check in a race one night, their spirits will be buoyed by the affirmation that, "There's always that opportunity of the next race. Or that the next two-year-old that comes into the barn might be 'the one.' "

20

GIRLS AND THEIR HORSES

I was an insecure, introspective little girl. The fact that I was horse-crazy meant that I had some respite from what I perceived to be the turmoil of my angst-ridden life. I remember that when I was about eight years old, my father would drive me out to the regional park up in the hills where for five dollars he could rent me a horse to ride for an hour. We weren't a wealthy family, so this was as close to a horse as I was going to get for many years. This weekend ritual was something special we shared, my father and I. While he paid the manager of the rent string, I'd scuffle about the stable in my corduroys and wait for the object of my desire to become available. His name was Windy. I'd request him every time and was willing to sit idly on one of the scarred and weathered picnic benches until the group of riders he was attached to ambled into the stable yard.

Now that I have the eyes of a learned horsewoman, I'm sure I'd find fault with Windy. Even back then, though, I couldn't help but notice he was slightly lop-eared; his ears poked out on either side of the rope halter he wore beneath his bridle. And I'm sure he was splayfooted, with tufts of matted hair on his fetlocks. But love, even for a horse, is blind. As a child enraptured with horses, I thought Windy was the most beautiful creature on earth.

For the hour that I rode him, I'd make believe he was mine. I'd pat him on his neck, where the brown hair was slightly crusted with a day's worth of salty sweat. Gentle words would coo out of my mouth in an attempt to ease the drudgery that was the life of a rent string conscript. As our band of riders wound its way along the trail and through the park, I would purposely lag behind the wrangler leading the way. Then I could nudge Windy with the heels of my canvas sneakers until he broke into his springy jog. My amber Shirley Temple curls would bounce around my head and over my eyes, and I would start to laugh until we jogged right back to our place in line. Occasionally fate smiled upon me, and Windy would tumble into a canter for a few strides. Oh, that would thrill me!

At the end of the ride, the wrangler would silently take the reins from my hands as I slid off Windy's back. A lead rope would be snapped to the little brown gelding's halter and he would be left tied to the hitching post, stoically awaiting his next rider. I always tried to console him, yet I knew there wasn't any hope that I could make good on my promise to treat him to a better life. When I'd leave, I'd turn around in the backseat of our Ford station wagon and gaze at Windy. The last glimpse I'd have was of him tethered to the post, dozing in the sun, oblivious that I was waving good-bye. There was an unrequited aching in my heart, for this was the first time I fell in love.

Though most horse-crazy girls eventually transfer their love of horses to a boyfriend and then to a husband, those of us terminally stricken never fully supplant a horse with a human. We may fall in love and take a spouse, but the bipedal human will never be worshipped with the same adulation as our four-legged horse. This is a cause of consternation for every man whose beloved obsesses over the quality of alfalfa her horse consumes but cannot perfect her domestic culinary skills past the level of frying ground beef. It's no wonder so many men, perplexed by this equine mania, are abandoned in a dazed state, strewn alongside life's roadway of love.

My girlfriend Corinne, who is admirably attached to her warmblood gelding, Willem, summed up one of her erstwhile relationships with a nonhorse man thus-ly: "Seven years ago I had a terrible spill from Willem. I had broken up with the love of my life a few months before, so a friend called him to let him know what had happened. A few years later we began dating again. At dinner he said, 'I can't believe you didn't get rid of that stupid horse after it tried to kill you.' That was followed up with, 'You love that horse more than you love me.' " Corinne, who in my estimation is never afraid to speak her mind, says she explained to the ignorant beau, "The horse was here before you turned up the first time. He was here when you left, he's still here, and he will be here when you're gone." This, as it turned out, is exactly what happened. Corinne dumped the guy. Again.

The man who remains persistent must ultimately accept that he'll never understand the attraction his woman has for a 1,000-pound beast. He can take comfort in knowing he is loved, but he must also resign himself to accepting that when she looks him in the eye and says softly, "I love you," it is not with the same ardor as when she utters that phrase to her horse. Maybe we just speak a different language of love to our horses. Corinne claims she has learned to speak a common dialect with Willem. "After over 10 years together, there's quite a vocabulary in signals and gestures and sounds. I look at the clock at 5:00 P.M. on weekdays, and I know that Willem is facing the back of his stall, looking out toward the parking lot, and waiting for my car. He whinnies with joy each day when I get there. And yes, he needs me."

Devotion like that is hard to find. Men can see what they're up against. There's simply no extinguishing the bond that girls of any age have for their horses.

LASSOING
LIFE'S LESSONS

The four horses gallop into the arena and make one lap in single file. The two Appaloosas and two paints make a flashy quartet, but their riders are even more dazzling. Dressed in red, white, and blue spandex with a dusting of scarlet sequins, they begin to perform maneuvers known in western horsemanship circles as trick and fancy riding.

To the casual onlooker, trick and fancy riding just look death-defying. Even the names given to the skills conjure up a flirtation with tragedy. There's one called split-the-neck and another one labeled the suicide drag. The horses seem to savor their participation in these skills with legs that fire like pistons against the ground and ears that pin back in earnest. Yet the riders are fresh-faced, doll-figured girls and young women, not brawny, hard-bitten cowboys. Put them in petticoats and add some taffeta and they'd make fine debutantes at a high society cotillion. And that's just the way the late Tom Maier, founder of Riata Ranch International, would want it.

Nearly 50 years ago, Tom began a program of horsemanship and character development for young riders, and his dream evolved into the Riata Ranch Cowboy Girls, who are world famous. "We like to teach the traditions and values of the American West," explains Jennifer Welsh. If as director and manager of Riata Ranch International she is the spokeswoman for the group, she is also a fine representative of the very lifestyle she champions. As casually as some suburban woman might flip open her handbag and whip out her cell phone, Jennifer snaps a lariat into action and spins it around her petite waist like a hula hoop.

Jennifer relates that she was drawn to the Riata Ranch program in 1974 when she was six years old. Her family had just moved to the central California town of Visalia, a community at the foot of Yosemite and next door to the little town of Exeter, home to the ranch. "I was immediately fascinated with the whole program. Not just the incredible riding feats, but the whole idea of getting to work with the horses, learning ranch skills, and also traveling and performing. It just seemed like something I had to do."

Opposite: The Riata Ranch Cowboy Girls live by the traditions and values of the American West. Left: Riata Ranch performers in practice.

A respected alumnus of the ranch and the trick-riding program, Jennifer is now what amounts to a combination riding instructor, head mistress, tour chaperone, and counselor on social graces. But most important, she strives to convey Riata's motto "Building Character Through Disciplined Instruction" on a daily basis. "I teach the girls that there is more to life than just being around horses. They have to be able to present themselves in public, to speak well, to be able to converse, to be courteous. They are ambassadors of our American western heritage and the United States."

Offering a testimonial of sorts is 13-year-old Shaye. A native of St. Louis, Missouri, she is expert at the riding tricks performed at a gallop. When I ask how she became a member of the troupe, she says she saw the Riata Ranch Cowboy Girls perform in her hometown and knew she had to find her way to California. Shaye relates how Jennifer teaches a life lesson each day in addition to riding skills. "She'll write a saying on the blackboard, and then we'll discuss it. We'll talk about how to apply it to daily life." As an example, a recent adage was *It's not the container, but the contents that matter.* "In other words," Shaye says with a note of reflection to her voice, "what matters in life is not the physical looks we're given or how we just appear on the outside, but how we conduct ourselves. How do we treat each other? How do we behave in public? Are we kind and polite?"

All this and they muck stalls, clean water troughs, and learn general ranching chores. "When anyone comes to the ranch, it's explained to them right away that part of the program is working on a ranch," Jennifer says. Perhaps the most mundane daily task is raking the barn aisle, which must be done religiously in a particular pattern. This continues Tom's philosophy that humans are creatures of habit

and that solid (if repetitive) work makes for self-discipline. Besides, the barn looks tidy and that builds self-respect and pride in one's environment.

Yet while the regimen seems strict, very few who make it through the initiation of the inevitable bruises and sore muscles ever want to leave. Though the program is designed

Opposite: The Riata Ranch gang.
Left: A Riata Ranch rider's activities range from mucking stalls to performing death-defying tricks in the ring.

"*We like to teach the traditions and values of the American West.*"

— JENNIFER WELSH

for girls and women ages 9 to 20, graduates often indoctrinate their own daughters into the program or become hosts for participants visiting from outside the area.

One of the main enticements is the chance for travel and to travel accompanied by other passionate horse lovers. Thus far, the Riata Ranch Cowboy Girls have performed all over the United States and in 17 foreign countries, including excursions to China, Israel, and Germany. "Sometimes the horses are flown to where we're performing," Jennifer reveals. But when costs are prohibitive, travel logistics are hectic, or quarantine restrictions create a snake's nest of red tape, the troupe borrows horses referred to them by the organizers of the event. When asked if that's a concern, that horses suitable for trick riding might not be an ubiquitous commodity, Jennifer laughs understandably and says, "Well, we like to have 30 days to work with the horses, to feel them out, and get them used to the routine. But sometimes we only have a week. Luckily, usually it all works out fine."

The requirements for a good trick-riding horse aren't all that specific. Foremost, he must be well broke and gentle so that he's not apt to spook and spurt off if something—errant child or blowing piece of plastic trash—distracts him. He must also gallop without much encouragement, stop abruptly on command, and then stand rock solid. Of course, he must do this all while a nimble human is dangling from his side or standing upon his back. It's rather amazing that so many horses accept such duty with nary a flick of an ear or a swish of a perturbed tail. But then there's Rocky.

"Rocky is too smart," remarks Jennifer. The Appaloosa gelding is 15 years old, so there's no dismissing his antics as due to adolescent whims. "He's very sensitive to his environment. He'll notice things outside the arena, like a kid running or a dog or something on the ground. Plus, being so smart, he tends to anticipate what comes next in the performance." Think of a whiz kid who already knows the answers, so he gets bored in class. "He can be tough." Not being one to back down from a challenge, and meeting both horses and humans on their own terms, Jennifer hangs onto the horse nonetheless.

As the group begins to head back to its encampment to freshen up for the afternoon performance, Shaye comforts one of the riders who sports a raspberry on her cheek and a blooming black eye. Her mount had stumbled for a few steps while she was outstretched from the saddle, parallel to the ground. When asked if safety is ever a concern, Shaye addresses the issue almost clinically. She offers that any sport, including snowboarding or football, can be dangerous. But, "we're so prepared. Everything is done step-by-step. By the time we get to this point, everything just comes naturally." The Riata program generally includes 25 girls at a time. The youngest and the most novice riders begin as assistants and helpers during performances. As they gain skills and confidence, they rotate onto the team. With so much indoctrination and education, mishaps are kept to a minimum. "I don't get nervous that I'm going to make a mistake," Shaye says, exuding poise that belies her youth. "I know I won't do anything wrong. And I trust the horse. But I do get really, really anxious before a show because I want everything to be beautiful and perfect. It's the things that I can't control, the unexpected things that might happen…" and she lets her voice trail off, perhaps preferring not to conceive that anything should ever go awry. And yet, that is indeed one of life's biggest lessons: sometimes the routine we planned to perform requires some improvisation. Certainly Jennifer will be conveying that bit of wisdom long before these girls ride off into the sunset.

Opposite: The Riata Ranch Cowboy Girls have performed in over 17 foreign countries.

chapter

22

A LIFE SPENT
WITH HORSES

"Yes, I shall continue to spend my life with horses. When I am old and wrinkled and gray, my horse won't care."

— CINDY HALE

I was only four when my father plopped me on the back of an ebony pony at the Los Angeles County Fair. I imagine he stepped back to watch my reaction. It was love at first ride. I like to think that my passion for horses was inborn, something basic to my genetic code, an instinctual drive that could not be ignored. To find a fountainhead for this passion, I have to look no further than my grandmother.

She was a petite woman with a head full of tight tiny curls and eyes that were bright and expressive. My favorite photograph of her is one in which she's all dressed up in a taffeta gown with a layer of gossamer fabric pleated about her waist. She has on a pair of ornate pearl earrings and there's an orchid corsage pinned to her dress. To anyone else she looks like a fairy godmother. But to me she was simply Grammie. Despite her finery, I know in my heart that she'd just as soon be wearing blue jeans, a plaid flannel shirt, and cowboy boots because Grammie was a horsewoman deep in her soul.

My earliest memories of her are sketchy at best. But she and my grandfather had once owned a large dairy farm. By the time I came along, they had moved to a small estate in the foothills of San Diego and grew avocadoes. Yet throughout the split-level house were signs that a former horsewoman lived there. Her horses were gone, but her love for them remained. She had a collection of small horse figurines made of china and porcelain. Each was unique. One that was glazed in mahogany brown sported green glass eyes. Another was a smoky gray Arabian with a black tail that ended in a curlicue. Every time I visited, Grammie would let me hold each one. I would do so gingerly. I was afraid I'd drop or chip one not so much because I recognized its value, but because I knew these were Grammie's treasures that reminded her of another life.

While my father was out at the lake fishing and my brother was playing army in the avocado grove, Grammie would entertain me with stories about her favorite horse, Dan. He was a big sorrel gelding with a sprinkling of white markings. I'm guessing now that he was part saddlebred or Tennessee walker because Grammie often remarked about what she called his single-foot gait. With a little urging she could get Dan into his animated, ambling walk, and they'd traverse the countryside all day long. She told me how she and her best friend, Caroline, would climb into the cab of the old farm pickup truck with my grandfather, and he'd haul them and their two horses to the head of a long trail that meandered across the hills. The two horsewomen would ride all day, camp out at night, then meet up with my grandfather on the other side of the pass, and he'd take the quartet home. On another occasion, she and two of her friends camped out in the mountains near Yosemite and rode through the pines and among the granite boulders, savoring nature.

The Christmas I was 14, Grammie gave me a box that contained Dan's bridle. Both the shanks of the bit and the buckle on the headstall were crafted with handmade silver hearts. I did not yet have my own horse (that would come later in the spring) but now at least I had a bridle. Yet the gift was more than that. I realized even then that she had bestowed upon me a memento she'd kept tucked away for many years, electing to bring it back into daylight only when she could pass it on to someone else who understood the magic of horses.

Now each time I cross paths with an older adult rider, someone whose face is etched by years spent in the sun, whose hands are knobby with calluses from holding reins or clutching a lariat, I think of Grammie.

Opposite: A passion for horses knows no age.

Above: Despite the finery she sometimes wore, Grammie had the soul of a true horsewoman.

mother to stop riding. The decision had nothing to do with the loss of her youth.

The allure of horses simply transcends any constraints of age. I've watched elderly people look into the eyes of a horse and it is as if two souls have linked up. The horse cannot ascertain age. But I believe a horse can recognize and comprehend wisdom. The older human, on the other hand, sees the horse as the manifestation of vitality. Though an aged person may not be able to kick up her heels, metaphorically speaking, the horse can do so literally.

I am certain that I will ride until I am no longer able to hoist my rickety body into the saddle. If and when I'm confronted with that situation, I shall ride around in a cart pulled by a large pony. I'd prefer a little palomino with a bushy flaxen mane, thank-you very much. I certainly refuse to shuffle into my golden years wearing velveteen slippers. My feet will be in boots.

Yes, I shall continue to spend my life with horses. When I am old and wrinkled and gray, my horse won't care. He'll still nicker to me for carrots. That I am the bringer of treats makes me forever the love of his life. He'll press his big flat forehead against my shoulder, feel my frailty, and gently nuzzle my arms with a caress of fuzzy gray lips. And when I lead my horse to the mounting block and coax my aging limbs into the saddle, he'll stand respectfully silent, not commenting on how I'm not quite as limber as in years past. Once I sink into the saddle, feel the stirrups stretch down to welcome my legs, and hear the creak of worn leather as I settle in, he'll turn his head softly to one side, glance up at me and I'll know what he's saying:

Pick up the reins now. We'll go for a ride. And I shall make you feel young again.

I like to imagine that if she'd had the opportunity, she would've kept riding even after the dairy farm and Dan had been replaced by an avocado orchard and three growing sons, circumstances that compelled my grand-